Educational Genocide

A Plague on Our Children

HORACE (ROG) LUCIDO

ROWMAN & LITTLEFIELD EDUCATION
A division of
ROWMAN & LITTLEFIELD PUBLISHERS, INC.
Lanham · New York · Toronto · Plymouth, UK

Published by Rowman & Littlefield Education
A division of Rowman & Littlefield Publishers, Inc.
A wholly owned subsidary of The Rowman & Littlefield Publishing Group, Inc.
4501 Forbes Boulevard, Suite 200, Lanham, Maryland 20706
http://www.rowmaneducation.com

Estover Road, Plymouth PL6 7PY, United Kingdom

British Library Cataloguing in Publication Information Available

Library of Congress Cataloging-in-Publication Data
Lucido, Horace, 1945–
    Educational genocide : a plague on our children / Horace (Rog) Lucido.
       p. cm.
    Includes bibliographical references.
    ISBN 978-1-60709-717-4 (cloth : alk. paper) — ISBN 978-1-60709-718-1 (pbk. : alk. paper) — ISBN 978-1-60709-719-8 (electronic)
   1. Educational tests and measurements—United States. 2. Education—Aims and objectives—United States. I. Title.
    LB3051.L83 2010
    371.260973—dc22   2010010941

∞ ™ The paper used in this publication meets the minimum requirements of American National Standard for Information Sciences—Permanence of Paper for Printed Library Materials, ANSI/NISO Z39.48-1992.

Printed in the United States of America

This book is dedicated to students and teachers whose lives are constrained under the oppression of high-stakes testing.

I am forever grateful to my wife, Vincie, who has supported my vision for forgiving teaching and learning.

Contents

Foreword

In February 2009, *Time* magazine reported Secretary of Education Arne Duncan's vision for America's children. The goal, he declared, is to expand standardized testing to the point where we can look every second grader in the eye and predict, "You're on track, you're going to be able to go to a good college, or you're not." Clearly, those who hoped that Barack Obama's presidency would usher in a new, more equitable, and humane era in the realm of education seem destined to disappointment. In fact, rather than diminishing the clout of test scores on the future of children, it appears the goal is to expand the current testing culture until we can line up little children and predict who will succeed and who is doomed to fail.

As Rog Lucido illustrates in his book, *Educational Genocide: A Plague on Our Children*, this notion of standardization assumes that all children come to school with equal ability, that they return to equally nurturing homes, and that all school facilities are equal as well. It also assumes that the teacher is the *only* factor in students' achievement as defined by their scores on tests. In fact, the goal now as articulated by Duncan is to create so expansive a database that the government can link test scores to individual teachers, thus paving the way for merit pay or, on the flip side, teacher firings. Thus, as Rog Lucido shows us, the roles of what it means to learn *and* what it means to teach are now controlled by abstract and distant forces outside the classroom.

Sadly, despite the many problems with test questions, scoring, interpretations, and applications that Rog documents, testing has nonetheless evolved into a monolithic force. While testing affects the future of virtually every student and teacher in the country, few of us are equipped with the tools to cut through the testing jargon and complex smokescreen that cloud the fallibility and inequities of standardized tests. As Rog Lucido shows us, human beings and human behaviors defy standardization. However, as a society we are seduced into treating test scores as if they represent absolute truths—even as we accede to the folly that we can definitively identify and quantify complex constructs such as intelligence and ability.

Unless we approach the current testing culture armed with knowledge, parents and teachers are destined to remain victims to its burgeoning influence. We are at risk of sacrificing the future of our children to what Rog Lucido exposes as a fallible process that has narrowed the curriculum and turned schools into test-prep factories as testing company giants have usurped the role of teachers as the scholarly and creative center of students' education. While many who care about education recognize that that Godzilla has its foot on our heads, too often, parents and teachers are either ignorant of the ramifications of testing on their lives or they lack the tools to talk back—and to fight back.

Again, that's where Rog Lucido comes in. In *Educational Genocide: A Plague on Our Children*, he sheds light on common testing complexities and the false promises of standardization; he tells it like it is. In doing so, we also see the chasm between what schools are and what they *should* be. Rog, with his background in teaching, gently and compassionately *teaches* his reader. He has a unique gift for explaining complex terminology in clear, uncluttered language so the reader comes away with a deep understanding, not just of the testing terminology and concepts, but of what they mean in *human* terms. And that is why his message sticks. He does not *just* tell us. Like any good teacher, he strikes a chord in us by showing the relevance of our new understandings.

I was also struck by Lucido's comprehensive knowledge of the testing culture and the literature surrounding it. This knowledge was hard won and is an outgrowth of his tireless activism as he's spoken and written about the dangers of high-stakes testing for years. This is not the voice of just one passionate person screaming from the abyss. What Rog does is pull together the voices of many others to build a clear, concise, and very readable book about standardized testing. With sharp intelligence and wit, he cuts through the complexities and confusing language that cloud the issues and disguise the dangers of the testing craze on students, parents, and teachers.

When I started writing this foreword in response to Rog's book, my first thought was that I understood more about testing now than I did previously. I wanted to explain how he helped me understand more about the procedures and the underlying premises that have fed the testing culture and enabled it to metastasize through the illusion of statistical and scientific certainty.

As I wrote, however, I realized that this book moved me. This is not just a smart book. It is also a touchingly personal narrative. Don't be fooled by the fact that this work is vital and informative. It is far more than that. It's genius and what makes it memorable is Rog Lucido's gift to speak to us, not just from the head—but from the heart as well.

Dr. Elaine Garan
Professor of Literacy and Early Education
California State University, Fresno

Acknowledgments

There is much gratitude to spread around. Of course, it all begins with my students, who have given me the inspiration to teach while preparing and writing this book. I continue to thank all of those educators, parents, and community members who have formed the foundation of Educators and Parents Against Testing Abuse (EPATA), Assessment Reform Network (ARN), California Coalition for Authentic Reform in Education (CalCARE), and the California State University Kremen School of Education. While these groups have been the soil where I have been most nurtured during the last five years of the preparation of this book, it is the individuals therein who have shared and enhanced my dreams for education.

It began when Susan Harman anointed me the Central Valley coordinator of CalCare, when I asked her how I could be of help. See what you started? Elaine Garan, who wrote the foreword, and Glenn DeVoogt of the Kremen School of Education provided continued encouragement and support during this process. I am so thankful for the following members of EPATA, who not only provided the persistent vision of what should be in education but also were willing reviewers of the original draft of this book: Helen Pitton, Linda Caffejian, Angelica Carpenter, Susan Schmale, and Brad Huff. Other reviewers of note include Jo Behm, John Walkup, Dianne Akoi, Amy Valens, and Marc Barlow. I am in awe of Gerald Bracey (now deceased), Susan Ohanian, and Monty Neill (FairTest), who have provided the national leadership and persistent challenge to the consequences of high-stakes testing. Their work continues to give me hope for a better future for students.

It goes without saying that I am indebted to publishers Rowman & Little-field Education, who saw value in this book through Dr. Thomas F. Koerner, vice president and editorial director. I am grateful for all the help Maera Stratton, assistant editor, provided with much of the detail work.

How can I ever repay my wife, Vincie, for her ongoing reading and commentary on each draft of this book, but more so for her daily sacrifices of time and energy to keep me focused by continually reminding me of the importance of this work? And finally for my son, Joseph, a current fifth-grade teacher, who is not only living in the current high-stakes testing atmosphere, but is willing to take risks by making his values known through his writings and activism.

I am humbled by the selflessness of all of the aforementioned in helping to make this book possible. It surely is a tribute to the hope contained within the human spirit.

Introduction

Adrienne worked hard at doing the math problems for her test. The teacher gave the children directions to copy the problems from the test sheet onto a piece of lined paper. There, they were to do the work and then copy the answer on the right edge of the original test sheet where an answer column was provided.

When I first saw the red F streaked across her paper I felt a rush of disappointment pass through me. I said, "Gee, Adri, what happened?" "I don't know, Daddy," she tearfully answered. "I thought I did well." "Let's sit down and look at these, honey, and see what you did wrong." As I surveyed her papers, the only correction marks I saw were on the answer column. Examining the problems associated with each red check, I found that she had made few mathematical errors.

Her major mistake was in recopying. For some of her "errors" she had transcribed the wrong numbers from the original sheet onto the lined sheet—but performed the arithmetic correctly. The other errors involved having done the problems correctly but transcribing her answers back onto the answer column incorrectly. Because of a learning disability, Adri has a visual-motor difficulty, of which her teachers were aware.

Yes, Adri did fail "transcription" on this test—but not mathematics. She suffered the humiliation of other students' comments about her grade as well as her own self-abasement because of the red F covering the front of her paper. If it were not for my inspection of what she had done, her self-perception would have been even further eroded. In writing a heated note to her teacher (one of my former students!), I asked him please to be more concerned about the nature and significance of his student's errors—not just the answers and resulting grade.

During this experience I thought to myself, "How often is this scenario repeated in other classrooms?" Even though this experience took place nearly thirty years ago, long before the high-stakes testing mania hit our schools, it illustrates some basic principles in discovering the truth about what a student knows and is able to do. There have been many times when a student has arrived at the correct answer for the wrong reasons and also students who have an incorrect answer but with a correct process and some minor transcription error, as my daughter had done. What I have found is that my students need timely feedback on what they are doing right, what they are doing wrong, and how to improve.

This cannot happen with superficial assessments. Correcting the "answer" is just the first step of a process that involves an evaluation of how they arrived at that answer. This can be done by asking students to justify answers with written reasoning, or by discussing their work with them, or a combination of the two. Wherever possible, students must be queried to defend their thinking. One assessment given at one point in time should not be the sole determiner of what a student knows and is able to do.

Multiple sources of evidence need to be employed to give the student an opportunity to demonstrate mastery in various ways. Classroom assessments, projects, presentations, portfolios, and mastery conferences are just a few such examples. Adri was not afforded any of these options. All she received was an F on the paper.

The instructor, too, needs timely feedback on how well classroom instruction and activities fared. This is necessary for both individual students and the class as a whole. Teachers are constantly modifying and adjusting instruction to fit both large-scale and individual needs. If multiple assessments are used, and these continually indicate which important concepts and processes are weak, reteaching with modification is necessary.

Individual students may do exceptionally well according to one assessment medium and poorly with another. Continuous monitoring could reveal learning disabilities and/or preferred learning styles. Adri's teacher did not teach another lesson on what was covered on the test. Adri was not pulled aside to see why she failed. Her grade was just recorded in a grade book.

Parents want to know how their children are progressing in school. They count on a valid and professional response to this basic request. Communication with their child and instructors is a critical component. Artifacts of student work and accompanying explanations to justify student evaluations are important aspects of this dialogue.

Adri's grade on this test did not begin to tell the story of her comprehension. Only a thorough evaluation of her work revealed the truth. Luckily, she has educated parents, native to the United States, who can analyze her work and point her in the right direction. What becomes of students who do not have this option in their family? Where do they turn? The attempt to summarize Adri's mathematical skills with one mark was misleading, incomplete, and failed in its purpose. Multiple sources of evidence with explanations would have painted a much more complete picture of her understanding.

The school site, district, state, and federal government want to know about how students like Adri are faring in school. They, too, want to know the truth. They believe that student test scores are the way to hold everyone accountable. Once student scores are collected, school and district aggregate scores are disseminated to the public.

Funding decisions and evaluations of teachers, administrators, schools, districts, and states are based on information received about individual student testing done once each year, mostly in a multiple-choice format. These one-time tests are called "high-stakes" because the scored results can prevent students from graduating, hold back students from advancing to the next grade, force students into remedial courses, and prevent students from taking elective and enrichment classes. In California and other states, students are labeled as advanced, proficient, basic, below basic, and far below basic from their score on one set of tests. Labels stick.

High-stakes tests modify what is taught and how teaching is to take place. They are redefining teaching as a process of just preparing students for these tests and little more. In education jargon we say teachers are reduced to "test prep." In preparation for the testing, districts are forcing teachers to follow line-by-line scripts, determining time on task by using paced lessons regardless of the capabilities or depth of understanding of individual students or the class as a whole.

High-stakes test results can terminate superintendents, eliminate principals, fire (reconstitute) entire staffs, and even strip away governing power of a school board when or if it is taken over by the state. High-stakes tests results can label schools as "underperforming" and/or "failing." High-stakes test results can even affect home prices in a given district. Wouldn't a prospective home buyer give a second thought to enrolling their child in a school that has been categorized as "failing"?

Test makers themselves, departments of education, and professional psychological and evaluation organizations continually state in one form or another: No single test can ascertain whether all educational goals are being met. A variety of tests—or "multiple measures"—is necessary to provide educators with a well-rounded view of what students know and can do. Just as different tests provide different information, no one kind of test can tell us all we need to know about a student's learning or higher-order thinking skills. This "multiple-measures approach" to assessment is the key to valid, reliable, and fair information about student achievement.

I just picked up a prescription for an antibiotic. I spoke with the pharmacist about when to take it and what I can or cannot eat with it. He had some very specific guidelines. If I don't follow them, I could get sick, and reduce or eliminate its effectiveness. He is a highly trained professional. I would be foolish to disregard this advice.

If the medication was for my child and I did not follow the precautions, I could be guilty of child endangerment. Not so with some lawmakers and some state and local educators. If these are the cautions and directions on the "prescription" of high-stakes testing, which our students are required to take, why are they not being followed? Why are we dispensing this medication without proper safeguards? Why aren't we thinking about the swath of disastrous consequences?

It is systematic abuse and educational malfeasance. It is arrogant and misguided to think we can get at the truth of legitimate, meaningful teaching and learning by relying heavily or totally on individual or aggregate scores from high-stakes testing. We think we can get at the truth by employing high-stakes testing and then summarizing this truth with the resulting scores. We permit teaching to prostitute its noble purpose by pursuing higher scores while misleading our students into believing that education is all about preparing for and taking high-stakes tests. Why are public figures, business leaders, and politicians encouraging this path?

As if this isn't enough, high-stakes testing infects our educational system with a culture of fear. Threats of what will happen to states, districts, schools, teachers, and students are central to maintaining control. Administrators fear for their jobs if scores do not improve. Teachers are afraid to speak out against policies and directives they know conflict with superior classroom practices and violate ethical standards for the teaching profession. Parents are cautious about talking to teachers and administrators about the impact of testing on their children. Who knows how their child will be treated following a complaint?

Business leaders are afraid that low scores will erode our international competitiveness and lower profits. In the end, all of this concern is foisted upon students who are pressured into learning for the sake of improving their test scores. These children fear what low scores can mean for their life. I don't like the thought of Adri or any other student going to school afraid. This system teaches students to value themselves in terms of their scores. Students quickly learn that their worth to the teacher and school is the scores they can produce.

In this climate, we relish in comparing this student to that, this school to that, this district to that, this state to that, this country to that. We create a system of winners and losers. Why is this mentality allowed to continue? What are the fundamental beliefs that support this path? How is all of this impacting the individual student? Adults created this mess. How can we get out of it? These are some of the fundamental questions addressed in *Educational Genocide: A Plague on Our Children.*

It is my intention not only to inform and convince you of the validity of the themes presented in this book but also to encourage you to begin a process of effecting change in the area of schooling in which you find yourself most involved. So, rather than read this book as you would listen to a song sung by a soloist, try to sensitize yourself to the voices of many singers as their voices join together in a prophetic chorus for change.

Oftentimes the call for genuine change must come from many different individuals and groups. Just as on the first warm night, when the sound of a solitary cricket soon triggers responses from others, so that one by one they form the evening chorus that says summer is here, it is my desire that you, too, can become a summer cricket as you find within these pages a hope, a challenge, and a sense of direction for change, as well as guidance and inspiration to join a growing call to action aimed at restoring meaningful teaching and learning in U.S. public schools. The elimination of high-stakes testing will once again free educators to teach for the ultimate good of all students.

1

Are All Things Measurable?

In man, the things which are not measurable are more important than those which are measurable.

—*Alexis Carrel, Nobel Laureate*

I love my wife. Do I love her to a 10? How about a 9.5? Or perhaps a 9.723? Wouldn't that be a great conversation? I could tell her how much I love her in terms of a number. Then she could tell me how much she loves me in like fashion. Then we could discuss the difference between a 9.723 and a 9.8776.

We humans have been talking about love for a long time. I suspect that long before there were written songs and poems, expressions of love surely adorned cave walls of ancient peoples. So by now we should have a pretty good handle on it. Over the years I am sure there have been many attempts to put love into a numerical scale—that is, to "quantify" it as we have attempted to do with intelligence (IQ). To take some complex concept of the human mind and try to simplify it to a singularity like a number or word is called "reification" (rā-ə-fə-kā-shən). In *The Mismeasure of Man*, Stephen J. Gould gives us an insight into understanding this concept:

> One of the fallacies—reification, or our tendency to convert abstract concepts into entities (from the Latin, res or thing). We therefore give the word "intelligence" to this wondrously complex and multifaceted set of human capabilities.

This shorthand symbol is then reified and intelligence achieves its dubious status as a unitary thing.[1]

IS IT POSSIBLE TO REIFY BY QUANTIFYING?

Can we make love into a number? The answer is a tongue-in-cheek "yes." Yes, if we believe we can first define love in terms of a finite set of understandable statements: Love is kind, love is patient, etc. Yes, if we take each of those statements and formulate them into a finite set of questions: Are you kind to your wife? Are you patient with your husband? (When you write a question that you believe fits the statement, it is called "alignment.")

We now create a test that includes that set of finite questions, say, one hundred of them. We then give the test to thousands of people and tally the number of "yeses" for each person and get a distribution of scores. Listing the scores ranked from highest to lowest follows this system. Some people will have one hundred yeses, some with none, and many more in between. Following this, we gather a group of people and show them the questions and the resulting set of thousands of scores, and then ask them to come to a consensus at which point in the distribution of scores will a person be said "to love."

This group may believe that those above that point (sometimes called a "cut score") are all lovers—say, seventy "yeses" is the cut score—and those below are not. So by this standard, you may think that finally you have a handle on love. You may decide that all who want to marry should be given this test before the ceremony; if either bride or groom does not make the cut score (70), the wedding is off.

You now have in your possession a testing instrument and a cut score that will forever change the lives of those individual couples who did not make the cut. Giving society what we believe to be a quantitative measurement of love would logically lead to administering this "love test" to all couples before marriage. Is this a good price to pay to make sure that those who scored 70 and above are truly lovers? Congratulations, you have just reified love; that is, you have made it into a unitary thing: a quantity, a number.

Love no longer needs to be discussed. We have terminated all engagement in love talk. Now that we can "measure" love with a number we can close the door on further dialogue. The question "He loves me or he loves me not?" becomes moot.

Many of those personal qualities that we hold dear—resilience and courage in the face of stress, a sense of craft in our work, a commitment to justice and caring in our social relationships, a dedication to advancing the public good in communal life—are exceedingly difficult to assess. And so, unfortunately, we are apt to measure what we can, and eventually come to value what is measured over what is left unmeasured. The shift is subtle and occurs gradually.[2]

WHAT WERE THE ASSUMPTIONS THAT MADE THIS SO EASY?

To begin with, we assumed that we could reify love; that we could make a complex entity into a simple thing, a number. How can you tell what can be reified and what cannot? When the degree of complexity approaches the infinite. Thinking about infinity can drive us crazy. Our minds cannot fathom such a limitless concept. We are bound by our earthly existence in such a way that takes away our ability to make concrete that which by its nature is not concrete. We symbolize infinity with a mark that looks like a sideways eight: ∞. We can symbolize love with a heart (♥). The elusive nature of human mental and behavioral attributes like infinity is mired in complexity and forbids reification.

It is like saying, "Love is so complex that I cannot possibly figure it out, so I will select a finite set of chunks of it, call the sum of those chunks love (an infinitely complex attribute), and reify each chunk—make those into numbers. Then I will conclude that I just reified and measured love." We humans do not like it when we cannot be certain. Doubt and ambiguity make us uncomfortable. So what we do is try to convince ourselves that we can erase all doubt and anchor truth securely by denying our fallibility and claim victory over a set of infinite descriptors. The thinking goes like this: "Certitude is better than doubt. Numbers are concrete while opinions vary."

OLYMPIC DIVING AS AN EXAMPLE

The goal in Olympic competition is to determine the best diver by ranking them by their diving scores.

> We now encounter the second fallacy: ranking. But ranking requires a criterion for assigning all individuals to their proper status in the single series. And what better criterion than an objective number?[3]

So to do this the Olympic committee selects seven experienced judges to score each dive on a 0–10 scale in increments of .5. So a typical dive could be a

7.5. The scoring rules throw out the highest and lowest scores and average the five that are left. The premise is that each judge can make the dive into a unitary thing, a number. Believing they can do it does not mean that they can. How can a judge absolutely distinguish between a 7.5 and an 8? Answer: they can't.

A dive consists of an enormously complex array of movements in approach, execution, and completion of the dive. The judging system feigns some type of scientific certitude. It settles for a number that suddenly takes the judge out of the picture (with all of his or her opinions about the dive) and substitutes a number.

The number gives the impression of objectivity but in fact is no different from a basketball referee calling a foul. It is a human judgment. Throwing out the highest and lowest score is not done for any mathematical reason. It is because the scoring rules want to attempt to nullify judges who are prejudiced for or against a particular diver based on their country of origin or other factors. Could the real truth of the dive be best represented by the highest score? Or perhaps the lowest? If each judge is considered equally fallible, why should the high and low scores be eliminated?

This reminds me of a related situation with the scholastic aptitude test (SAT). A student can take it many times before high school graduation. The SAT process assumes that the highest score is the one that best represents the student. This is the score that is then sent to the student's university of choice. The SAT process does not throw out the highest and lowest. Assuming the scores do have validity, the higher score is no more valid than the lowest. In fact, the lowest score could be the truer representation of the student's knowledge. But numbers don't lie . . . or do they?

FALLACIES OF SCORE CALCULATION

Once numbers enter the picture, our minds move quickly away from the quality of the dive and fixate on the score. We begin with a set of scores that only claim accuracy to the nearest .5, and after averaging and multiplying by another number called "the degree of difficulty," suddenly a diver's score is accurate to the nearest .01. Here is an example. Let's say after throwing out the highest and lowest scores there are five to be averaged: 6.5, 7.0, 6.0, 7.5, 6.5. The average becomes 33.5 / 5 = 6.7. This is then multiplied by the degree of difficulty of the dive, say, 1.4 ($6.7 \times 1.4 = 9.38$). What is wrong with this process?

First, the original judges' scores are good only to the nearest .5. That is, a judge cannot score a 6.4, 6.6, 6.7, and so forth. It has to end in either a .5 or 0. Judging is only good to the nearest .5. So 6.7 is not a possible result. The errors continue when the scoring process multiplies the 6.7 by the degree of difficulty, 1.4, and you arrive at 9.38. Now this number is accurate to the hundredths place—9.38. It implies that the score has become more accurate than when it began.

In reality the score can be no more accurate than the *least* accurate value (all the judges' scores must end in a .5 or 0). The final score should therefore be 7.0 × 1.4 = 9.8, and rounded up to 10.0. The problem with this is that the scoring process may not discriminate between two divers whose final scores are 10.0 or any number to the nearest .1 (for example, if both had a 9.3).

To make it more possible to choose a winner, the scoring process makes two measurement blunders. It arrives at an average of 6.7, when the scoring is only good to the nearest .5 (33.5 / 5 = 6.7), and should be rounded up to 7.0. Then, when multiplying by the degree of difficulty, the 9.38 becomes more accurate (to the hundredth place) than either of the numbers used in the calculation (6.7 × 1.4 = 9.38).

Making these same errors on everyone's score does not make the outcome correct. This is where "two wrongs" are forced to be a "right"! All of this demonstrates that once we attempt to take a quality of complex and indefinite proportions and reify it into a quantity—a number—the science, fairness, and even ethics surrounding the consequences are neither justified nor valid.

VALIDITY IS DETERMINED BY INTERPRETATION

The study of statistics is based on what to do once you have the numbers. It assumes that the numbers are valid. In fact, numbers in and of themselves can never be valid. Score validity is based only on the appropriate interpretation of those numbers.

> Well, technically it's not the test that's valid or invalid; rather it's the inference made about a student, based on the student's test performance. . . . Although a test may be described as reliable or unreliable, because reliability focuses on the consistency with which the test does its measurement job, it (the test) can never be valid or invalid. Again it's the score-based inferences that we make about a student or a group of students that are valid or invalid . . . in reality, all they know is how to respond to a particular set of items: those in the sample. Validity vanishes.[4]

The numbers take on meaning only when a human tells you what he or she believes that the numbers mean. When humans tell you about numbers, they are telling you the truth as they see it. This is called *interpretation*. I can tell you that although my wife and I can both see the 77° reading on our thermostat, her experience is too warm; mine is just right. The number does not change, but the interpretation does.

After all, who can complain when the 9.38 diver beats the 9.37 diver? This system attempts to be scientific when it is not. It pretends to be objective when it is not. Numbers do lie when interpreted, portrayed, and utilized inappropriately.

> The fervor for this kind of standardized testing reinforces the kind of ranking games that are a particular enthusiasm of Americans and are certainly not unknown in other countries. We're willing and eager to rank anything—from the 100 greatest movies to the 250 best cities in which to raise children. Never mind that the criteria for such rankings are hazy at best; if we can't put a number on it and rank it, then what good is it?
>
> Numbers seem scientific and technological. So we test and test and test, oblivious or resistant to the possibility that standardized literacy testing often produces numbers with about as much utility or connection to reality as ranking songs on the old American Bandstand television program. "It sounds good, has a good beat, and I can dance to it. I give it an 87."[5]

OF STATEMENTS, QUESTIONS, AND CUT SCORES

Another assumption underlying attempts to reify love is that makers of the "love test" have sufficient experience and credibility. Considering the infinite number of statements we could possibly make about love, we assume that we chose the most important hundred. Since we are the test makers, shouldn't we have confidence that we know what is important about love and what is not? But this is not possible. We do not qualify as experts in love since we couldn't have possibly taken our own test. It's not even made up yet.

Is it possible that if others chose a different set of statements (love is confusing, love is painful, etc.), there would be another set of questions on which their test would be based? Could we ever select the perfect one hundred questions? Does it make a difference? Oh, no matter, maybe a different 70 percent would get married. Some couples will always end up disappointed; and that is just the way it is.

How about that cut score of 70? Are we confident that we have genuinely captured the truth of what it means to be a lover? Should we be concerned about those who would have been lovers if we had selected 68 or those who would no longer be lovers if we had selected 72?

EXTENDING REIFICATION TO OTHER DOMAINS

Since reification of love—that is, quantifying love—was so easy, do you think that we can score battlefield bravery? Adult compassion? Childhood generosity? Third-grade English? Eighth-grade mathematics? All we need are a set of statements (standards), a set of multiple-choice test questions that flow from those statements (aligned), a set of scores, and a cut score. Voilà—a done deal!

> It's not how high they jump or how fast they are—it's how they play football. You can't measure "will" and you can't measure "heart."[6]

Over the past hundred years there has grown a cult of people who believe that if you cannot measure something, then it does not exist. They believe the "something" has value because it possesses some sort of intrinsic property we can reify by quantifying, that is, make into a number. A good example of this is a district superintendent's statement in a document intended for all educators in his district: "In fact, one of our common sayings is 'If it can't be measured, it didn't happen.'"[7]

SEE IF YOU CAN REIFY BY QUANTIFYING

Often, teachers write commendations to students with a word or two across the top of their papers. Below are ten such words that are often used. Assign each word a whole number between 1 and 10 so that the one with a "10" is the best comment a teacher could write and "1" is the worst: Terrific/Fabulous/Wonderful/Great/Impeccable/Outstanding/Awesome/Superb/Perfect/Amazing.

Now have a few other family members or friends try it. You have just quantified these ten words. Compare your responses to others and then check at the end of this chapter for the correct answers. (Hint: there are none!) What do you conclude? Try as we may, we cannot determine with certainty or prove any one-to-one relationship between these descriptors and any number. They defy quantification.

Yet some would say that they have no existence because they cannot be quantified. But to the student these comments are valuable because they describe the *quality* of the assignment according to a teacher. They communicate the overall response of the teacher to this student's work. The teacher's emotion almost comes through. Why isn't the comment enough?

I know I have often used these exclamations with my own children: "That was a great throw!" "You did wonderfully in the play." They really seemed pleased and they clearly understood my judgment of their activity. Words, tone, body language, and the context genuinely convey what we value. Numbers strip away the human exchanges that give meaning. Words and expressions reveal elements of human thought and feelings that numbers cannot.

> So long as there is no science of politics in sight, attempts to substitute counterfeit science for individual judgment not only lead to failure, and, at times, major disasters, but also discredits the real sciences, and undermine faith in human reason. . . . To demand or preach mechanical precision, even in principle, in a field incapable of it is to be blind and to mislead others.[8]

WHERE NUMBERS DO AND DO NOT BELONG

Over the past five hundred years, man's ability to measure various physical and biological attributes of our world has led to amazing discoveries and contributed significantly to the progress of civilization. By applying these measurements to the industrial revolution of the late eighteenth and early nineteenth centuries, we began to see how important numbers used in measurement could be.

The use of numerical analysis by the business community contributed to its success. Our standard of living increased. We began to believe that the use of numbers had been so successful in science, industry, and business that real truth could be found only by using numbers. This confidence grew, and the use of numerical measurement was no longer confined to science, industry, and business, but applied to anything considered to be measurable.

> In her history of education research, Ellen Lagemann (2000) suggested that during the 20th century, education had a "romance with quantification" . . . that was reflected in its penchant for counting, measuring and calculating in order to resemble the hard sciences as closely as possible.[9]

Using multiple-choice IQ test scores to rank and order military personnel prior to and during World War I and World War II was concurrent with the testing of immigrants while we decided whether or not to admit them into our country. In the minds of some, this made sure we did not allow too many with "subnormal" intelligence to dilute our American population.

Since the growth of public schools quickly followed industry's need for an educated workforce, the idea to measure students' knowledge was not far behind. After all, like the example attempting to reify love, children have been around long enough for us to take them with all their complexity and simplify what they know and are able to do into a set of numbers.

Students' knowledge and skills cannot be reified, boiled down to a few numbers. Like the concept of infinity, humans are too complex. Knowledge and skills are too complex.

> We are talking about a worldview in which any aspect of learning, or life, that resists being reduced to numbers is regarded as vaguely suspicious. By contrast, anything that appears in numerical form seems reassuringly scientific; if the numbers are getting larger over time, we must be making progress. Concepts such as intrinsic motivation and intellectual exploration are difficult for some minds to grasp, whereas test scores, like sales figures or votes, can be calculated and tracked and used to define success and failure.[10]

STATES' STANDARDS VARY AND ARE UNBOUNDED

So what the high-stakes test maker does is to ask the state to develop a finite set of statements called "standards" that describe what is to be learned by the student. Here is one set of standards for third-grade English in California:

Comprehension and Analysis of Grade-Level-Appropriate Text:

2.2 Ask questions and support answers by connecting prior knowledge with literal information found in, and inferred from, the text.

2.3 Demonstrate comprehension by identifying answers in the text.

2.4 Recall major points in the text and make and modify predictions about forthcoming information.

2.5 Distinguish the main idea and supporting details in expository text.

2.6 Extract appropriate and significant information from the text, including problems and solutions.

2.7 Follow simple multiple-step written instructions (e.g., how to assemble a product or play a board game).

Here is a similar set of third-grade English standards from Texas:

(9) Reading/comprehension. The student uses a variety of strategies to comprehend selections read aloud and selections read independently. The student is expected to:

(A) use prior knowledge to anticipate meaning and make sense of texts (K–3);

(B) establish purposes for reading and listening such as to be informed, to follow directions, and to be entertained (K–3);

(C) retell or act out the order of important events in stories (K–3);

(D) monitor his/her own comprehension and act purposefully when comprehension breaks down using such strategies as rereading, searching for clues, and asking for help (1–3);

(E) draw and discuss visual images based on text descriptions (1–3);

(F) make and explain inferences from texts such as determining important ideas, causes and effects, making predictions, and drawing conclusions (1–3);

(G) identify similarities and differences across texts such as in topics, characters, and themes (3);

(H) produce summaries of text selections (2–3);

(I) represent text information in different ways, including story maps, graphs, and charts (2–3);

(J) distinguish fact from opinion in various texts, including news stories and advertisements (3); and

(K) practice different kinds of questions and tasks, including test-like comprehension questions (3).

Here is a mathematics set from California eighth-grade Algebra I:

Students solve multi-step problems, including word problems, involving linear equations and linear inequalities in one variable and provide justification for each step.

Here is a similar Algebra I set from Texas:

A.5) Linear **functions.** The student understands that linear functions can be represented in different ways and translates among their various representations. The student is expected to:

(A) determine whether or not given situations can be represented by linear functions;

(B) determine the domain and range for linear functions in given situations; and

(C) use, translate, and make connections among algebraic, tabular, graphical, or verbal descriptions of linear functions.

I could, likewise, do comparisons for each of the fifty states. You can see that even within parallel learning domains, the standards are varied and unbounded. They contain both similar and different components. Thus, the questions used to develop state high-stakes tests will vary accordingly.

The fact that standards vary from state to state and from one revision to the next confirms the fact that there are no absolutes in educational testing, just differences. These differences are a healthy sign of diversity resulting from cultural and historical factors that are at play in any human endeavor. Any attempt to "standardize" standards is an attempt to eliminate creativity and uniqueness of states, districts, schools, and students. Life would be rather boring with the availability of just one type of car, one type of food, one TV station, and one type of person.

ALIGNMENT OF STANDARDS TO QUESTIONS IS FICTITIOUS

A few years ago I was selected to go to an Educational Testing Service (ETS) training session for the selection of physics questions for their California Standardized Testing and Reporting (STAR) testing. ETS has the contract to produce the STAR tests. There were about ten or so teachers in the room. One physics standard was given to us and we were to spend the next hour developing as many questions as we could that we believed were associated (aligned) with that standard.

I came up with five. Given more time and more physics teachers, we could have come up with thousands of questions for that one standard. The state committees that wrote the standards could have created thousands of them. The narrowing of the choice of standards and the choice of questions for those standards is used for construction of STAR multiple-choice tests. Professor Emeritus George Hein further clarifies this point:

> But the essential point is that there is no objective way of selecting questions in the standard format of current testing regimes. That's one little realized crucial flaw of psychometrics. The practitioners of this art can provide exquisitely detailed analyses of the validity and reliability of items compared to other items and tests, but the very choice of any item in the first place is the issue. That they are "aligned with the standards" is simply a statement.
>
> No one, to my knowledge, ever provides any empirical evidence, based on experimental work that would let me know what "alignment" means in a quantitative way. Items are generated by a process that has no theoretical basis and no experimental base that adheres to the kind of "scientific" rigor that the tests are supposed to exemplify.
>
> There are no objective definitions of "bias," "culturally sensitive," "racism," etc., against which test items could be measured to apply a quantitative standard of the validity. So how can the tests actually assign cut-off scores, levels of progress, etc? In science, if you end up with a quantitative result, you're supposed to have an unbroken chain of quantitative experimental data that justifies doing so.[11]

HOW DO STUDENTS' SCORES MESH WITH REALITY?

How much time will the students have to answer the questions? How many questions could we ask in that time? The state and federal governments pretend that this process of arriving at a number for each student's knowledge and skills is valid. It's not. The arbitrary nature of time determination and number of questions dismisses the nature of variability in student brain processing times and pretends that the testing time window and number of questions is a nonissue, when in fact it is a critical component in student responses. Students' having the same amount of time and number of questions does not mean equal opportunity.

> There has been much discussion about a recent study showing that drugs used to treat clogged arteries have a puzzling effect. People who take them lower their cholesterol levels: that all-important number is improved. We would expect that this lower cholesterol would result in better health, but the research has revealed that in spite of the better number, the arteries remain clogged and the heart disease unimproved.
>
> Doctors are saying that we are "treating the number," rather than the actual illness. Parents and teachers are asking the same thing about standardized tests. For years, we have been "treating the numbers," seeking to increase standardized test scores, assuming a solid connection exists between these scores and the educational health of our students.[12]

It is much easier to quantify the number of times a semicolon has been used correctly in an essay than it is to quantify how well the student has explored ideas in that essay. Thus, the more emphasis that is placed on picking standards that we think we can quantify, the less ambitious the teaching will become. We will only teach what we believe we can count.

CONFIDENCE?

As the result of the each state's high-stakes testing program, parents, students, teachers, and schools will receive a set of scores. How much confidence should you have that the reification of a student's knowledge and skills into a set of numbers is possible? None.

> Over the last two weeks, Kim Karesh, spokeswoman for the Tennessee Education Department, has repeatedly been asked by reporters about the big discrepancy between Tennessee state scores and federal scores. "I've asked these questions myself to federal officials, and the answers don't make a lot of sense," she said. "In education these days, we talk numbers until we're blue in the face. But there's a bigger philosophical question: 'Can you really boil it down to a number?'"[13]

If not numbers and scores, how are we to assess what students know and are able to do? How do we get to the truth of the matter? Read on.

A high school principal once told me, "You don't grow the cow by weighing it." It's time to put away the scales and start improving the nutritional content of the feed.[14]

2

Objectivity Is Subjective

The researchers Marguerite Lederberg and George Fitchett recognize this problem in an interesting article with the provocative title "Can You Measure a Sunbeam with a Ruler?" . . . The point of their title is to reiterate a longstanding concern in science: the difficulty of quantifying human experience. By attempting to measure a sunbeam and in so doing reduce it to that which can be quantified by a ruler, we lose the character of the sunbeam itself. While such measurement may be possible, it cannot capture the essence of the sunbeam and in fact may distort it.[1]

—*Richard P. Sloan*

Impartial and objective: two very powerful words. Often we believe we want objectivity, but do we really? Consider this scenario: A highway patrol officer pulls me over for driving over the speed limit. I hope he would just give me a verbal warning, but he does what he believes objective impartiality dictates. He writes out a ticket.

Even though I explain that I am rushing to school because my son was seriously hurt in gym class, the officer chooses not to take that into consideration. If he took *my* situation into account and instead opted for a warning, the officer thinks that he would be preferential and subjective. He just may treat the next driver he pulls over in a different, inconsistent fashion.

If I believe the "law is the law," then there is no wiggle room for extenuating circumstances or even a possible functional error of the radar gun. If there is any weakening of his judgment of certitude he does not want to show it. No excuses, no thoughtful deliberation, and, for sure, no compassion.

OBJECTIVITY IN GRADING?

Here is a common classroom dilemma: Students are called up one at a time to be shown their total score and grade for the semester. The score for an A (announced at the beginning of the year) is 90 percent or higher. The student has an 89 percent. What should the teacher do? Should every other student who has an 89 percent be treated in exactly the same way? How about the student who has an 88.7 percent? 87.8? Should the teacher have wiggle room to modify the grade?

Do we want all teachers to be impartial and objective? Is it acceptable for the teacher to just say, "I am *trying* to be impartial and objective?" How about just posting students' grades or, better yet, have students wait until the report card comes out? In this way the teacher can minimize the personal interaction and be less liable to sway from the 90 percent boundary for an A.

Listening to students' responses to their scores and grades can be risky. At grade time some teachers wish they could be robotlike machines, dispensing grades in an emotion-free atmosphere so the appearance of impartiality and objectivity can be maintained.

If impartial objectivity reigned, the couple that wanted to get married but did not make the love test cut score described in chapter 1 should have no recourse. They cannot wed. Their score is 68. Passing is 70. Can we make this distraught couple believe that their "love test" was given and scored in an impartial, objective way?

NUMBERS, HUMAN BIAS, AND THE TRUTH

Numbers impose on our minds a false sense of objective truth. We deny the significance of humans making up statements about love, of humans constructing the questions, of humans deciding on a cut score, all of the most critical aspects of the testing endeavor. The entire process is mired in subjectivity. But somehow, high-stakes test proponents want to convince the world that all personal bias and preferences have been eliminated from the meaning of the score. The concealed sanitation of our human frailties suddenly elevates our choices from unreliable subjectivity to the illusion of a noble and respected realm of objectivity.

A pass percentage is a bad standard for educational progress. Conceptually, "proficiency" has no objective meaning that lends itself to a cutoff.[2]

We latch onto whatever numbers are thrust upon us and push aside all the inherent variability that comes with humans who construct the tests, administer them, and ultimately evaluate the meanings of the scores. Those who espouse high-stakes testing would like us to believe that this process is the pinnacle of objectivity, that is, "scientific." They are wrong.

THE SCIENTIFIC PROCESS AND GENERALIZABILITY

Modern scientific investigation dates back to the time of Galileo. This process begins with making observations about the world and then guessing as to why it is so. The result is called a hypothesis. Next, the researcher must examine the nature of the observations to determine if they lend themselves to qualitative or quantitative investigation. The researcher then designs an experiment to determine the truth or falsity of that hypothesis. They do the experiment, gathering qualitative or quantitative data. They analyze that data—most importantly, by taking errors into account. Finally, they draw a conclusion that affirms or denies the hypothesis.

The research report is then presented to peers (usually via journals) to judge the validity of the conclusion(s). Others attempt duplication of the results by using similar or alternate experimental designs to see if indeed they come to the same conclusion(s) and whether or not those conclusions are "generalizable" (i.e., can this one experimental result prove applicable everywhere?). Generalizability is a critical component of research results.

THE "SCIENCE" OF READING?

As an example, let's consider the quest to discover the "science of reading." Are reading programs that claim to be "scientifically based" generalizable? The U.S. Department of Education currently approves funding for only materials and programs that it interprets to be "scientifically based." It does not address the question of whether the tenets of the scientific process can be applied to validating any given program. It assumes that all educational methods have the potential to be scientifically supported, when in fact this is far from the truth.

Writing a law that labels a narrow methodology scientific does not make it so.[3]

One of the major flaws in the attempt to discover the "science of reading" lies in the belief that one can give evidence that, if a reading program "works" with large groups of students, it will, therefore, work for each individual student. In order to appear scientific, such reading programs attempt to standardize instruction, so repeating the identical process should lead to the same results on each individual.

Many of these programs are scripted and paced. All the teachers have to do is to read exactly what the program says within a specified amount of time. The belief is that if the teacher follows a step-by-step procedure, similar to reproducing a successful experimental process that was done elsewhere, the results will be the same: All students will succeed. It doesn't happen.

> "We have choices," Cummins asserted. "A lot of folks at higher levels in the hierarchy don't want you to know that you have choices because the dominant model of school improvement that is being inflicted in many states as part of the No Child Left Behind reading-first approach is to impose what is viewed as a scientifically supported approach to instruction and to wipe out teacher choice, to make it as teacher-proof as possible."[4]

REAL SCIENTIFIC EXPERIMENTATION AND EDUCATIONAL PROGRAMS

In the "hard" sciences, such as physics or chemistry, one can follow a standardized prescription to do x, y, and z in separate trials to achieve a "physical entity," and the same results should follow. That is, the "physical entity"—say, pure water—experimented with in San Francisco can be reproduced in many locations around the world and by many researchers, so that all of its attributes at the outset are nearly identical and the results of experiments on it are reproducible.

Not so with the human person. In fact, each student is unique. So the educational process that worked with a distribution of many individuals (some did well, some were average, and some fared poorly) in Milwaukee cannot be predicted to work with a single individual in Houston. Accepting that results with Milwaukee students will yield identical results in Houston schools describes the false scientific mindset applied in education. Such mass-scale generalizations refuse to acknowledge individual student differences and their unique responses to the same input.

One of many reasons to have high regard for teachers in the classroom is that they can modify instruction to best address the uniqueness of each student rather than follow a canned, one-size-fits-all program that purports to be scientifically based. So those who attempt to find the "science of reading" and other such educational "sciences" begin their quest without really understanding the limits of generalizability and the nature of standardization in genuine scientific inquiry.

REAL SCIENTIFIC EXPERIMENTATION AND HIGH-STAKES TESTING

This same type of misinformation is often applied to the use of high-stakes testing. Much of the public believes high-stakes tests tell the truth about such critical life-altering milestones as eligibility "readiness" to graduate or teacher competence, because the public naively believes such tests are scientifically objective. They are not. The researchers and educators who design and interpret these tests do have partiality as to the outcomes. Their experimental design, data, analysis, and conclusions are often prejudiced by what they hope the results will validate.

In short, it is assumed that the high-stakes testing enterprise is not an exercise in becoming a self-fulfilling prophecy, but it is. There are biases. Researchers and educators are humans, not machines. They bring their personal history to their work. They are not without partiality and therefore are not objective. The myth of claiming scientific objectivity is a fallacy in denying human conscious and unconscious preferences at each step in the design and development of any educational program.

> Rather, I criticize the myth that science itself in an objective enterprise, done properly only when scientists can shuck the constraints of their culture and view the world as it really is. . . . But science's potential as an instrument for identifying the cultural constraints upon it cannot be fully realized until scientists give up the twin myths of objectivity and inexorable march toward truth. . . . The second reason for analyzing quantitative data arises from the special status that numbers enjoy. The mystique of science proclaims that numbers are the ultimate test of objectivity. . . . If—as I believe I have shown—quantitative data are as subject to cultural constraint as any other aspect of science, then they have no special claim upon final truth.[5]

FDA, AEA, AND PROFESSIONAL STANDARDS

If a pharmaceutical company wants to prove that the laboratory results of a new medication show great promise, they are required to present their findings to the Federal Drug Administration (FDA) for permission to test on humans. The FDA reviews the research and either grants or denies permission. This is the initial peer review process.

Following human testing, once again FDA reviews the experimental results, and if approved, the drug can be marketed. There are always precautions (possible errors) regarding interaction with other drugs, side effects, and potential negative consequences of use. The prescription is issued under the guidance and dosage of a medical professional. The patient (or responsible adult) can choose to follow the physician's directions or not.

Is it wise to take a drug not approved by the FDA? This professional organization has both the staff and the legal authority to monitor appropriate safe use of drugs. Otherwise, an unsuspecting public could harm themselves by taking drugs outside professional medical oversight and review. Likewise, in the educational field there is a professional organization whose policies and precepts set the standards for educational testing. It is called the American Evaluation Association (AEA). It issues guidelines and standards but has no legal authority to approve or deny the use of high-stakes tests. AEA guidelines, developed from a respected body of educational scholars and psychometric experts, should be incorporated in any large-scale testing policies, especially high-stakes tests with the potential for negative life-long, irreversible consequences affecting hundreds of thousands of students and teachers annually. Unfortunately, many state education agencies ignore AEA recommendations.

Violations of AEA Guiding Principles and Other Professional Standards

Evidence of the impact of high-stakes testing shows it to be an evaluative practice where the harm outweighs the benefits. Many high-stakes testing programs

- invoke a fallible single standard and a single measure, a practice specifically condemned by the Standards on Educational and Psychological Testing;
- are implemented and used to make high-stakes decisions before sufficient validation evidence is obtained and before defensible technical documentation is issued for public scrutiny; and
- are employed without credible independent meta-evaluation.[6]

HIGH-STAKES TESTING LACKS CORROBORATION

Students are forced to take the high-stakes testing medicine. In some states, parents can opt their students out of some of the testing. There is no other legal oversight to protect their best interests. The high-stakes testing "experiment" is based on an unproven premise: *A once-a-year set of multiple choice tests accurately reflect the truth of what an individual student knows and is able to do.*

This is the major presumption that drives the entire testing mania. No corroborating evidence supports this statement. No other experiments are conducted to verify if conclusions based on high-stakes test scores are valid. There are no multiple sources of evidence to justify any results or inferences about what an individual student or group of students know and are able to do.

Students are not required to justify or explain their answers. Other forms of assessment are precluded: student presentations, portfolios with reflections, research papers, classroom assessments by teachers, projects, mastery conferences, and the like. The testing is high stakes because decisions about students, schools, districts, and states are made on this unproven construct.

DON'T JUDGE BIG BROWN BY ONE RACE

In 2008, Big Brown won both the Kentucky Derby and the Preakness by five lengths. But when the next test came, the Belmont Stakes, the last of the Triple Crown, he came in dead last. So what do we believe about Big Brown and what he can do? If I refuse to consider the Kentucky Derby, the Preakness, and any other races he ran, is this a proper way to evaluate Big Brown?

Should the Belmont Stakes tell the whole truth about him? It was later discovered that he had a cracked hoof, probably as a result of improper shoeing. High-stakes testing does not take into consideration all the other "races" students participate in throughout the year, but only their final "Belmont Stakes."

YOU CAN'T ADD APPLES AND ORANGES

What state and national governments would like to "measure" about student learning is not measurable. "Is this a measurable quantity?" is the first question any scientific hypothesis must address. Are high-stakes test scores measuring the truth about my child's learning in school? True measurement requires the use of units: feet, pounds, seconds, kilograms, meters, and so on. It is clear that there are no "units" attached to the right or wrong answers tabulated on these high-stakes tests. One inch plus one inch is two inches. Inches and inches are identical units, so you can add them. One inch plus one pound makes no measurement sense. They are different units. One measures length, the other weight.

For example, in the English portion of a high-stakes test, one question may deal with one facet, such as writing, while another deals with a different aspect of English, such as reading. To add one question's correct response to the other means that they are the same facet, which they are not. Even on a very basic level, any score, which is the sum of correct responses, becomes scientifically inappropriate. You are adding different units.

What is worse is pooling answers dealing with diverse skills, such as algebra, probability, and geometry. Each question is an independent—a "test" unto itself and not a measure. One cannot legitimately add up correct responses to unrelated questions. They do not have any relationship to each other. When scores are inappropriately tallied, the reported numbers try to assert that some performances, or people, have more of "something" than do others. What is that "something"? It's a nothing.

MEASURE THE *MONA LISA*?
Can anyone measure the *Mona Lisa* as a work of art? You can measure its length, width, and thickness. You can determine its mass and the frequencies of colors it reflects. But as an art connoisseur you can talk about it and describe it, but not measure its artistic and aesthetic values. These are not entities that lend themselves to measurement. You have one *Mona Lisa*. You can believe you are measuring it. You can think you are measuring it. But that does not mean that it is really being measured. Test makers think they are measuring something, but they are measuring nothing.

INTERPRETATION AND ERRORS
The possible side effects and cautions with the results of pharmaceutical research and patient use are clearly disclosed to the patient and doctors. This is a transparent portion of the "errors" possible with the use of the medication. But the errors contained in high-stakes test scores for each student and school are not revealed, described, or explained to those who receive the scores. The numbers appear to be perfect and final. They are not.

Error analysis in science is a major component of experimentation. It can either support or reject any anticipated conclusion. Invalid interpretations of the numbers that high-stakes test constructors collect are not transparent. There is a strong belief that those who read and draw conclusions from scores (students, parents, teachers, school boards, legislators, and the public) do not have the capacity to understand the implications of the scores' measurement errors.

Test score distributors do not want to reveal the possible side effects and cautions that should be considered in the use and misuse of their numbers. They do not want to cast doubt on the conclusions they and others draw from their data.

> Theories are built upon the interpretation of numbers, and interpreters are often trapped by their own rhetoric. They believe in their own objectivity, and fail to discern the prejudice that leads them to one interpretation among many consistent with their numbers.[7]

ERRORS AND A HIGH-STAKES TEST

Assume a high school student scores 348 on his high school exit exam; 350 is passing. The test he took has an inherent scoring error that shows a probability of varying eight points on either side of the student's score, a sixteen-point range. This is called the conditional error of measurement. So the student's true score could be as low as 340, or as high as 356. With this latter score the student would pass.

The conclusion by the state does not consider the calculation of errors in the decision as to whether or not a student can graduate. They consider the passing (cut) score of 350 as errorless, perfect! They claim that this is objective, scientific, and just. It is none of the above. The vast and harmful consequences of disregarding random and systematic errors are an egregious fault and omission of responsibility.

Scientific measurements are done many times over and wherever possible use different methods and techniques in order to support and justify any conclusion. Students take a set of tests once a year. Then students, parents, educators, and state and national offices of education come to invalid inferences, and they use them to make decisions about students, schools, teachers, and districts. These decisions are touted as scientifically objective. They are not.

> Substantial measurement errors exist in any research design, Loftus adds, because a multitude of uncontrollable influences impinges on a person's nimbleness with

numbers or whatever else the experimenters decide to study. "Social scientists have embraced null hypothesis tests because they provide the appearance of objectivity," he contends. "But such objectivity is not, alas, sufficient for insight. [It provides] only the illusion of insight, which is worse than providing no insight at all."[8]

MEASURING DEVICES ALTER MEASUREMENTS

Are there other errors that are not put into numerical form that should be considered? For example, it is a fundamental principle that whenever scientists measure any entity by introducing a measuring device, the mere introduction of the device modifies the event being measured. A thermometer placed into a beaker of water changes the temperature of the water—the very thing it attempts to measure. The test is no longer attempting to measure what knowledge or skills are in your child's head, but now includes the effect that the test itself might have on her ability to express that knowledge or skill.

How often have you heard or personally experienced the statement "She just doesn't test well"? In thirty-eight years of teaching, I can't tell you how often I have taken aside kids whom I considered to be good students, and queried them on a concept they missed on a test, only to find out that they had a clear understanding of the idea but that they just "froze" or "forgot" under the stress of testing.

Do the test makers calculate any error assigned to this principle of interference? No. Each student has his/her own unique response to the test that affects the thinking process and hence the resulting scores. The error could be minimal; the error could be immense. Simplistically, test makers see the testing instrument only as it interacts with an objectified human brain, not with a real person.

TESTING SETTINGS AND SYSTEMATIC ERRORS

In its document "Key Elements of Testing/Test Measurement Principles" (May 2004), the California Department of Education asks this critical question: "Are the test results valid for the stated purpose and in the particular setting where the test is to be administered?"

Messick's Educational Measurement[9] states that the particular "setting" includes the student's own physiological, mental, and emotional condition, test, teacher, time of day, room, and school. There is no way to calculate an error for any of these "settings." Why not? How do you quantify the effect of a depressed student on his/her test score? How do you quantify the effect of an ill student on his/her test score?

Also, students who are absent during testing are required to take the test when they return to school. The students typically go to a designated room. This room, the teacher supervising the test, and the other students being tested are, clearly, much different from the standard conditions classmates experienced. These situations create an unusual setting and significantly alter the standardization, yet the scores are reported and interpreted as if nothing exceptional occurred. It is assumed that with thousands of students taking these tests, these "errors" just balance out. They don't. These errors impact individuals, but the scoring mechanism has no way to take these into account.

But the truth is that individual scores to individual students are reported, and no systematic error consideration is given to their particular setting. Because the calculated random error is based on large numbers of students, it is assumed that this error applies to individual scores equally. These random calculated errors are the *minimum* amount of error on individual scores.

Just because you cannot calculate an error does not mean it does not exist. These are called systematic errors. It indicates that something is wrong with the system of measurement; that is, it is either measuring the wrong thing or using the wrong instrument. Measuring your height on a bathroom scale is a systematic error. These systematic errors have the potential to overwhelm the purported measuring process and make it null and void. It is assumed by the test makers that students, like the tests, are "standardized." Everything is perfect. This is a false premise.

The truth is that high-stakes testing crusaders do not care about the outcomes on individual students; all they care about is the illusion of perfect score reporting. Many give this illusion power over how they perceive students, schools, and teachers. This misinformation feeds inappropriate judgments, policies, and practices that confine and restrict genuine student learning.

OBJECTIVITY AND HUMAN JUDGMENT

One cannot expunge the subjective nature of the high-stakes testing regime and pretend that the tests are "objectively scientific." The plain truth is that we must treat all student evaluations as a product of human judgment with all of its inherent strengths and weaknesses. Human judgment, despite all attempts to corral it, fails in its ability to provide perfectly reproducible results.

Our judicial court system is based on the deliberation of fallible humans. In the extreme, cases of life and death hang in the balance. Referees' subjective judgment calls in sports are filled with sometimes split-second responses that can determine wins and losses, successes and failures, with millions of dollars and reputations in the balance.

TEACHERS AND STUDENT EVALUATION

For nine months of each academic year, teachers communicate with their students about their progress. These educators play the role of judge, coach, and referee in ongoing assessments and evaluations using many different sources of evidence: homework assignments, projects, experiments, presentations, classroom responses, tests, quizzes, portfolios, mastery conferences, and the like. All of these interactions are subjective.

Instructors can and should take each child's mental, emotional, and physical health into consideration with each and every assessment. There is no such dynamic with high-stakes testing. So who can best tell parents about their children's educational progress? The teachers.

> After all, we turn to physicians and attorneys for their expert evaluations. Why shouldn't we expect education professionals to play a similar role?
> . . . Worse, even some teachers have come to trust test scores more than their own judgment. They have been served a steady diet of test scores from newspapers, politicians, and top school officials and led to believe that this is the logical way to monitor students.[10]

Although our educational system is mandated by state and national law to employ high-stakes testing, the vast majority of the public does not buy this as the optimal way of determining student progress. In a recent AP poll[11] the following question was asked: In your opinion, which is the best way to measure student achievement? See table 2.1.

Table 2.1. Which Is the Best Way to Measure Student Achievement?

	General Population	Parents
By means of test scores	28%	30%
By classroom work and homework	70%	69%
No answer	2%	2%

*Numbers have been rounded and may not add up to 100.

American citizens seem to get it. Hopefully, this book will help public policy decision-makers and state and local education leaders to get it.

STANDARDIZED TESTS ARE NOT SCIENTIFICALLY OBJECTIVE

Test makers attempt to convince society that they are being scientifically objective. They pretend that they can compare scores from many different locations across the state because all students are taking the same test. The test makers presume the conditions under which the test is to be taken are uniform. The same test taken under the same conditions means that the test is standardized.

While the test may be identical, the conditions under which the test is taken are far from equivalent. In the real scientific world, when many different scientists validate an experiment in many different locations, they must replicate the experiment under the nearly identical conditions of the original experiment.

We say the boundary conditions must be the same. The quantity to be measured must be under the same condition in all locations. In high-stakes testing, the only thing that is standardized with the administration of these tests are the test booklets, administration directions, and multiple-choice scoring that follows.

The most obvious and critical "nonstandardized" entity is that students who take the test do not all have equal states of mind, such as mood, anxiety, and indifference. Also, they arrive with various states of body, such as tiredness, sleepiness, and hunger. Students are human beings. They all have different personal experiences they are dealing with that affect them, not the least of which is their feelings about the test itself and its possible impact on their lives.

There is much evidence that these tests make some kids anxious and sick (see chapter 7). Another critical "nonstandardized" issue is how the time of day impacts student alertness. Student brains do not all wake up in the same fashion or by the same clock.

> Professor Foster said that forcing teenagers to turn up to school in the morning could result in more errors, poor memory, reduced motivation, and depression. Allowing secondary school pupils a lie-in on the other hand would improve performance in key subjects like English and math. "It is cruel to impose a cultural pattern on teenagers that makes them underachieve," he told a conference at the University of Wales in Cardiff. "Most school regimes force teenagers to function at a time of day that is sub-optimal and many university students are exposed to considerable dangers from sleep deprivation."[12]

Not only are the students' personal issues not standardized, but testing location and condition also are not. Classroom lighting, appearance, background noise, and air quality all affect students:

> The first, Daylighting in Schools, which was completed for Pacific Gas and Electric in 1999, examined school districts in three states. In Seattle, Washington, and Fort Collins, Colorado, where end-of-year test scores were used as the outcome variable, students in classrooms with the most daylighting were found to have 7 percent to 18 percent higher scores than those with the least. In San Juan Capistrano, California, where the study was able to examine the improvement between fall and spring test scores, we found that students with the most daylighting in their classrooms progressed 20 percent faster on math tests and 26 percent faster on reading tests in one year than in those with the least.[13]

> Poor indoor air quality (IAQ) has also been linked directly to low test scores, a disturbing fact given the high-stakes consequences of the Exit Exam. Studies have identified high levels of carbon monoxide, high temperature and humidity, low levels of natural daylight, high background noise, and overall building age and decay as factors that all result in lower student scores on performance and achievement tests; research has consistently found a difference between 5 to 17 percentile point of the achievement of students in "substandard" buildings versus those in "above-standard" buildings, when controlled for socioeconomic status of students.[14]

Even though all the test proctors are supposed to read and follow the directions in the exact same way, they don't. Their inflections and emphasis differ. Accommodations and modifications vary even within the same school, let alone among thousands of schools and districts within the same state. Some schools offer snacks before and between tests; others do not. Some schools offer prizes and incentives to students. Everything is supposed to be standardized, but it is far from that.

SCIENTIFIC TESTING FAILS ITS OWN TEST

These gross nonstandardized discrepancies do not lend themselves to calculating an error in individual student test scores. All conditions are assumed to be perfect and identical. They are far from it. On this fundamental issue of standardization on which supposedly valid comparisons of student test scores are grounded in science, the state's compliance with "scientific" principles fails miserably. There is no equality of high-stakes testing context and hence no justice in trying to make comparisons or defend the correctness of each student's test score.

Yet U.S. culture clings to standardized literacy tests as a means of providing meaningful information about students, teachers, and schools because such tests offer the illusion of scientific rigor (as well as those all-important quantifiable numbers) to an endeavor that ultimately can't be measured in a lab and for which numbers are meaningless. This infuriating numbers game allows politicians and media pundits to make facile judgments and cynical proclamations about education that they turn into a relentless cycle of testing, criticism, and punishment.[15]

3

Test Score Addiction

All addictions follow a similar pattern, and test score addiction is no different. Understanding this pattern for common addictions to drugs, food, and alcohol will help us see test score addiction more clearly. Recovery is possible. One successful process involves a twelve-step program. Each step is intended to support the addict in a path to health. While the disease of addiction will always be with them (just as treatable diabetes is for some with that disease), if addicts follow the steps, they can become symptom free.

ADMITTING POWERLESSNESS

The first step is without a doubt the most difficult. Addicts begin on the road to recovery by admitting their powerlessness over the use of their "drug of choice" (e.g., alcohol, food, gambling, pornography, spending). This admission says that once they begin to behave compulsively and find that they cannot stop using, cannot stop eating, or cannot stop gambling, they are exhibiting addictive behavior.

What's the matter with addictive behavior? It consumes the afflicted. It is all they think about. How do I get my next drink, my next lotto ticket, my next pill? This fixation blots out the rest of the world. They become isolated. All their relationships eventually fall away. They often lose their possessions, their jobs, and worse, their self-respect.

Unchecked, addiction can lead to lawlessness, incarceration, bankruptcy, and premature death. Addicts cannot be convinced by logical arguments that they are sick. The love of family and friends cannot dissuade the addict from their behavior any more than one can convince a person with a chronic disease to give it up for the sake of the family.

It doesn't work. It is only the addict who can begin their recovery by hitting bottom, by admitting their powerlessness over their drug of choice. It is a collapse of sorts—an implosion of personhood that leaves one in the greatest state of need. The addiction has consumed everything of meaning, and the person has no one and nothing to turn to for help.

RESPONSES TO ADDICTION

Often, those closest to addicts will look at addictive behaviors and excuse them as just a flight of fancy, a "thing" they are going through, something they will outgrow, or something that will soon be over with. After all, is it really that bad? Pretty soon it will be over and things will be back to normal.

The truth is that life will never be the same again. There has been a change, and with that change everyone in the relational sphere of the recovering addict will change, whether they admit it or not. So relatives and friends need a recovery plan. They need to deal with the impact of the addictions of their loved ones and seek health and healing.

The twelve steps provide that opportunity. As part of that process, family and friends need to look back and see what blinded them from seeing the addiction. Why were the addict's insane behaviors unacknowledged? How were family and friends getting some of their wants fulfilled by unconsciously supporting the addiction (codependency)? Recovery can transform addiction into an agent of change for the better.

HIGH-STAKES TEST SCORE ADDICTION IN AMERICA

Many in America have become addicted to high-stakes test scores. This addiction is supported and encouraged by our business culture and our local, state, and national governments.

> The term "maelstrom" captures all too accurately the reality of this test-obsession. . . . Thousands of American educators find themselves caught up in a score-boosting obsession.[1]

In the movie *Jerry McGuire*, an athletic agent's client shouts to him during a phone conversation, "Show me the money!" In short, "Enough of the talk; money is the bottom line; produce the right number and we will sign the contract!" We have become a culture that is satisfied with the education of our children only if we see the right numbers.

We have had various types of testing in America for many years. What is the difference now? Some people can drink socially for years before they become alcoholics. It's a gradual process of overextending the use of alcohol to such a point that it becomes more important than relationships. This overindulgence becomes an unchecked compulsion, an obsession.

The resulting behavior can be manic: an irrational set of actions that are directed at the acquisition of more and more alcohol. An addict is born. The addict wakes each morning with only one question: How will I get the next drink, pill, or obsessive fix? Whether it's alcohol, drugs, food, or high-stakes test scores, the addicts' compulsion becomes the focus of their life.

> We are ruining brains. Brain development is perhaps the most pressing reason why we need to rethink our current high-stakes testing mania.[2]

ADDICTION'S COLLATERAL DAMAGE

In all addictions, the impact on family, coworkers, and friends can be disastrous. Interactions and conversations can become combative. Fear runs rampant. The only thing that will satisfy the addict is more of his/her compulsion. They cannot see or experience the collateral damage done to those they love and care about. In their attempt to try to "fix" the addict, family and friends are often at odds with each other, saying and doing things far outside their character. Normalcy can become consumed by insane behavior, which Einstein defined as "doing the same thing over and over and expecting different results."

HIGH-STAKES TEST SCORE ADDICTION IN EDUCATION

A newspaper editorial says that "the exit exam is to do what it was supposed to do: put pressure on schools and students to improve performance." School districts flex their muscles by announcing administrative reassignments intended to scare principals into whipping their students and teachers to improve performance. And how is performance defined? Test scores, test scores, and more test scores.

Not surprisingly, America's near obsession with standardized testing has had a chilling effect on educational reform. In *Testing in American Schools*, a comprehensive 1992 report on the subject mandated by Congress, the U.S. Office of Technology warns that standardized testing is an enemy of innovation and that it threatens to undermine many promising classroom reform efforts.[3]

Those who support this type of mentality have either become test score addicts or are codependently nurturing another's addiction. They are frantically using their drug of choice, test scores, looking for the high that big numbers provide. They use fear to control each teacher as agents who can possibly satisfy their thirst for high scores.

Instructors can be chastised, threatened, and demoted for not following policies and practices that they know are harmful to their students. Many of these policies and practices are both contrary to state teaching standards and codes of ethics as well as supportive of the quest for high scores. Many teachers are afraid to speak out against these educational malpractices. Teachers pass this stress onto their students, pressuring them to perform well on the tests for the sake of high scores.

The relationships between teachers and students are being severely damaged. Part of the fallout of addiction is the destruction of relationships, as it is here. This is one of the signs that test score addiction is active. Teacher-student interactions become strained as students find that the scores they produce are more important than who they are as persons. As educators become so focused on improving test scores, they no longer even recognize when genuine learning is taking place.

School districts do not seem to care that teachers are leaving the profession over the demand to focus on students' achieving high scores. They do not care that students are getting sick over these tests. Relationships between teachers and principals are growing tense, as are relationships between principals and their superiors. Test score addicts' myopic view of assessment is poisoning our kids' desire to learn, squelching teachers' joy, and perverting education.

The problem is that once-a-year assessments have never been able to meet the information needs of the decision-makers who contribute the most to determining the effectiveness of schools: students and teachers, who make such decisions every three to four minutes. The brief history of our investment in testing outlined above includes no reference to day-to-day classroom assessment, which represents 99.9 percent of the assessments in a student's school life. We have almost completely neglected classroom assessment in our obsession with standardized testing. Had we not, our path to school improvement would have been far more productive.[4]

POWER, CONTROL, AND TEST SCORE ADDICTION

The insidious thing about this situation is that those who are most addicted to scores are also those in control, who have the power to legislate change: governors, legislators, school boards, and superintendents. They get support from some in the business sector whose quantified data driven enterprises have infected our schools. They get support from those community members and educators who place false confidence in these test scores and just want a quick and dirty numerical answer to the question, "Is my child doing OK?" They justify their addictive disease by claiming that this type of testing is necessary to keep the schools accountable.

The story goes like this: Public funds are being given for education, so prove to us that you are using the money to improve student learning. Evidence of student learning is defined only in terms of aggregation of student test scores. If you do not show improving scores, we will initiate sanctions to punish you.

Just as businesses set sales quotas, we will set arbitrary numerical benchmark target scores, so students, schools, and districts can be categorized. Each benchmark score will separate students into groupings such as advanced, proficient, basic, below basic, and far below basic in California. (Student classification nomenclature varies from state to state.) Schools will have to make their target scores or be considered underperforming and/or failing. Students will be labeled according to their level of proficiency. The drive to reach target scores feeds on fear-induced policies and programs aimed at each school, teacher, and student.

ADDICTION FEEDS IRRATIONALITY

Active addicts behave irrationally. They will do anything for their next fix—whether it is drugs, alcohol, food, gambling, or higher test scores. Their behavior is crazed, and this is what drives many to question their rationality, lack of compassion, and malfunctioning common sense. These behaviors are not normal. The pressure is on educators. The addicts or those under their control are sometimes driven to cheat on test results.

Some acquire answers through devious means and pass them on to their students. Sadly, there are teachers and principals who doctor student answer sheets. Groups of low-performing students have been transferred to other schools. Poorly performing high school students are forced out of schools to improve aggregate test scores and graduation rates. Good administrators and teachers are threatened, demoted, or fired because of low test scores under their watch.

> The allegations late last year that New York City teachers and principals had helped students cheat on standardized tests brings yet another wrinkle to the concept of high-stakes testing. Some say cheating is an inevitable result of an accountability system that ties jobs, bonuses, and school accreditation to test scores. "It should surprise no one . . . because of the enormous pressure on educators to produce better results," said author Alfie Kohn in a recent *New York Times* article. And this pressure doesn't apply only to New York. In Houston, a principal and three teachers were forced to resign when evidence showed instructors were prompting students during the state's achievement test. Kentucky, Rhode Island, and Connecticut have also had cases of test tampering or cheating in the recent past.[5]

DECEIT, DENIAL, AND ADDICTION

What is often said of active addicts is that "if their lips are moving, then they are lying." Deceit is central to addictive behavior—anything to keep the alcohol, drugs, sex, food, or test scores flowing. The worst lie is, of course, denial, as they try to convince themselves that nothing is wrong. They reject the observations of others about their behavior and substitute whatever is necessary to keep themselves using.

Doctors often report the incredulousness of some patients who are told that they have a serious disease when they feel just fine. But that is not the truth. The truth is that unless treated they could soon die. It is also true that many family and friends prolong the addict's use by also denying that there is a problem. If they acknowledge that their loved one is an addict, then they might have to change their own behavior and confront the addict with the truth of how their behavior is affecting those around them.

Parents, community members, and educators alike are responsible to inform those test score addicts of how their conduct is impacting students. Those addicted to high-stakes scores often deny the negative impact that testing has on students, teachers, and schools. "Accountability" becomes the shield that blinds them from seeing the consequences of their obsession for higher scores.

TEST SCORE ADDICTION, PROFESSIONALISM, AND COMPASSION

Should students who speak and read very little English be required to take these tests? Should students who are tired and/or malnourished be required to take these tests? What if they are sick or are having a personal or family crisis? Should students with learning disabilities be required to take these tests? Should refugees from Hurricane Katrina who moved to other states be required to take these tests? Should students who are crying with trepidation be required to take these tests? Should students with none of the above be required to take these tests?

In an ordinary classroom, teachers have a professional obligation to treat each student as an individual. They are to modify and adjust their daily lessons to respond best to their needs. In the high-stakes environment, an individual student's condition holds no value. There is no line in the directions for the tests that asks the teacher to assess the physical and psychological readiness of each student to engage in hours of testing. Compassion, understanding, flexibility, and common sense are barred. These human professional sensitivities challenge the illusions of scientific standardization and perceived objectivity.

Scientific research does address protecting students' rights. The National Research Act of 1974 is intended to safeguard human subjects so that researchers would have to:

- Protect the rights and welfare of the subjects.
- Assure appropriate methods of informed consent.
- Determine acceptable balance of risks and benefits.
- Shield information obtained and recorded in such a manner that human subjects cannot be identified, directly or through identifiers linked to the subjects; any disclosure of the human subjects' responses outside the research could not reasonably place the subjects at risk of criminal or civil liability or be damaging to the subjects' financial standing, employability, or reputation.[6]

The use district, state, and national researchers make of data mined from high-stakes testing is common. Students and/or their guardians are not granted informed consent about the ramifications of high-stakes testing. In some states, parents can opt their children out of some of the testing by law, but all parents are not afforded the opportunity to sign a consent document *before* testing is permitted.

The welfare and reputation of students are not protected, as test scores are posted on "data walls" in some schools and classrooms by numerical (and in some cases named) identifiers. Often, awards are given in the classroom for high-scoring students, thus identifying those who score lower by elimination. These harm students' developing self-worth and desire to learn. How is their welfare being guarded when the stress of the testing itself and the anticipated consequences traumatize some students before, during, and after high-stakes testing?

ADDICTION, SELF-MEDICATION, AND SUPPLIERS

Addicts have a hole in their psyche, an emptiness that they are trying to fill. That emptiness causes pain. Drugs, food, alcohol, and high test scores all anesthetize the pain. So test score addicts self-medicate by seeking high test scores to mitigate their angst. In this quest, they show little compassion for students and teachers. They lack the ability to take into account the conditions of students, to empathize or at least sympathize. Genuine understanding and sensitivity are avoided to prevent students and coworkers from seeing their soft side.

The test score addict's public persona must appear objective and non-compromising. Therefore, the perceived objectivity of scores is their drug of choice. Whoever continues to cooperate with the needs of the active addict does nothing more than prolong his/her addiction. And high-stakes testing companies do just that. They are the suppliers.

> The national obsession with performance and measurement means a booming business for test-producing and grading companies. In 2005, CTB/McGraw-Hill, Educational Testing Service, Harcourt Assessment, Pearson Assessments, and smaller firms generated $2.8 billion in revenue from testing and test preparation, according to Boston-based research firm Eduventures LLC. No Child tests alone produced about $500 million in annual revenue in 2005–06.[7]

LEARNING WITHOUT HIGH-STAKES TESTING?

Is it possible for a child to obtain a great education without high-stakes testing? The high-stakes testing addict says no. They believe that without these tests, teachers could not teach effectively, and students would not have the desire to learn. For them, scores and their consequences should be the only educational driver. It is the process of preparing for a once-a-year multiple-choice test that means something to these test score addicts.

They have no confidence in a teacher's desire to teach without real or implied threats. There is no confidence in a student's desire to learn without being motivated by the fear of failure. As long as there is cooperation from those who prepare students for testing, those who administer the tests, and those who take the tests, the test score addict will continue to get his/her fix. Those who stand idly by and watch the educational resulting carnage prolong this addiction to high-stakes test scores and resulting consequences.

RECOVERY'S REQUIREMENTS

The only solution for this high-stakes testing obsession is recovery. Dr. W. James Popham is a noted UCLA professor, the author of twenty books and 180 journal articles, and past president of the American Educational Research Association. He headed a group that built high-stakes tests for more than a dozen states. He has come to state:

> During the last three years, I've been trying to make up for my sins of omission. Having been raised in a religious home, I understand the payoffs of doing one's penance. But I need help from other educators who are also in the penance paying mood. We must take action to halt the harm that unsound high-stakes assessment programs are doing to our children. . . . I am, in fact, a *recovering test developer* [his italics].[8]

The addict has to stop using—either on his/her own volition or by being denied their drug of choice. To begin recovery, the addict must go through a time of withdrawal. High-stakes testing must stop. One path to stopping it is for those who facilitate any aspect of this testing regime to refuse to cooperate with a peaceful "No more." Just say no.

This decision means choosing to cease enabling addictive high-stakes testing behavior by denying addicts the scores. Peaceful noncompliance has its consequences. Anyone who has denied an addict money to purchase drugs understands this. Their responses can become violent and irrational. If you are not helping them, then you become an obstacle to their cravings and may suffer their emotional and physical wrath.

Here is a sampling of what has happened to some teachers and students who have said no to high-stakes testing:

North Carolina Special Education Teacher Doug Ward

After explaining his reasons for refusing to give the test in a May 12 e-mail to Jackson County school officials, including Principal Nathan Frizzell and Superintendent Sue Nations, Doug Ward was called into Frizzell's office the next day and asked to reconsider his decision. When Ward declined, he was told to pack up his things and head home that same day—suspended with pay. Nations declined to give specifics on the matter, as personnel issues are confidential, but she did say all Jackson County School Board members have been notified about the situation.[9]

Carl Chew and the WASL

Carl Chew, a 6th grade science teacher at Nathan Eckstein Middle School in the Seattle School District, last week defied federal, state, and district regulations that require teachers to administer the Washington Assessment of Student Learning to students. "I have let my administration know that I will no longer give the WASL to my students. I have done this because of the personal, moral, and ethical conviction that the WASL is harmful to students, teachers, schools, and families," wrote Chew in an e-mail to national supporters.

School District response to Mr. Chew's refusal was immediate. After administrative attempts to dissuade his act of civil disobedience had failed, at the start of school on the first day of WASL testing, April 15, Mr. Chew was escorted from the school by the building principal and a district supervisor. Mr. Chew was told to report to the district Science Materials Center where he was put to work preparing student science kits while district administration and attorneys consulted on an appropriate penalty for what was labeled, "gross insubordination."[10]

New York Intermediate Students Say No

More than 160 students in six different classes at Intermediate School 318 in the South Bronx—virtually the entire eighth grade—refused to take last Wednesday's three-hour practice exam for next month's statewide social studies test. Instead, the students handed in blank exams.

Then they submitted signed petitions with a list of grievances to school Principal Maria Lopez and the Department of Education. "We've had a whole bunch of these diagnostic tests all year," Tatiana Nelson, 13, one of the protest leaders, said Tuesday outside the school. "They don't even count toward our grades. The school system's just treating us like test dummies for the companies that make the exams."[11]

DENY THEM HIGH-STAKES TEST SCORES

Ending high-stakes testing will involve pain and suffering. The test score addicts will do whatever they can to coerce cooperation. Threats and retaliation are common ploys of addicts who are denied their drug of choice. If there is no one to prepare students for testing, no one encouraging students to prepare for tests, no one administering the tests, and no students taking the tests, the addicts will have the opportunity to take a first step to recovery.

When elimination of scores enables them to encounter the insanity of their need, they will then have the opportunity to admit their powerlessness over this addiction. Recognizing its existence is a crucial aspect to beginning the process of treatment and recovery. Their eyes will be opened to see what their addiction has done to themselves and others. Then they will seek reconciliation with those whom they have affected.

The school report cards came out in June. Rocky River Middle School passed the 2008 Ohio Achievement Tests, earned an Excellent rating from the state, and met the requirements for Annual Yearly Progress. For all of those accomplishments, Principal David Root has only one thing to say to the students, staff and citizens of Rocky River: He's sorry. Root wants to issue an apology. He sent it to me typed out in two pages, single-spaced. He's sorry that he spent thousands of tax dollars on test materials, practice tests, postage, and costs for test administration.[12]

TOWARD RECOVERY: RELATIONSHIPS WITH STUDENTS

What will help heal this addictive craving to quantify learning? The answer, of course, is meaningful relationships with students. Only those who can enter into this bond can see beyond the scores and tests to each individual person, and his/her hopes, dreams, and aspirations. Interacting with students in the classroom can be the therapy that opens the eyes of those addicted to high-stakes scores.

It can replace their need for numbers with a priority concern for kids that will help fill a void. This is the source of educators' passion: a love of kids. Without recovery, the high-stakes test score addict will continue to use, and our society will suffer the consequences of creating adults who have not been trained to think, but just fill in answer bubbles.

Pop quizzes, spelling bees, and the three letters that strike dread into high school students across the country—SAT. We have become a Test Nation, and the results can determine the course of a student's life. Some are beginning to question: Is it all too much? Has our obsession with testing pushed students too hard? Just what do tests really tell us?[13]

4

Accountability Is Corrupted

When I married my wife, I made a vow to her. I promised that I would love her from our wedding day forward, in good times and bad, for richer or poorer, through sickness and health until death. Not too many words, but a lot of responsibility. She could call me on my promise to be accountable for any actions or inactions that violated that vow.

Upon initiating their practice of medicine, many doctors take some form of the Hippocratic Oath:

> The practice of medicine is a privilege, which carries important responsibilities. All doctors should observe the core values of the profession which center on the duty to help sick people and to avoid harm. I promise that my medical knowledge will be used to benefit people's health. They are my first concern. I will listen to them and provide the best care I can. I will be honest, respectful, and compassionate towards patients. In emergencies, I will do my best to help anyone in medical need.[1]

Other professionals, such as engineers, real estate sales brokers, bankers, and lawyers, are supposed to follow a code of ethics and behavior tailored to their chosen fields. Parents, on the other hand, take no oath nor are they required to make a promise regarding the health and well-being of their children. But as their children's primary teachers, they are accountable. They have to live with themselves in taking responsibility for the messages they give their children in word and deed.

Some parents believe that this responsibility comes to them from their creator, and in that they are accountable to another, more prominent being. In this aspect of their parenthood, they are also legally answerable to the society and culture in which they live. They are to do all in their power to educate their children in becoming fruitful participants in their community. Once parents realize that they are limited in what they can teach, they pass a portion of this responsibility to teachers. They say, "I have and will continue to teach my children what I can but I want you to teach these other things I do not believe I am capable of teaching."

ARE TEACHERS ACCOUNTABLE?

To whom were your teachers accountable when you were in school? To whom were Plato, Socrates, Confucius, and Einstein accountable? To whom do present-day teachers have to answer? To whom are they bound to give an explanation for their work? They are first bound to themselves and their values.

Teachers are bound to speak the truth to students, parents, and the community. Truth is a function of their experience as educators. In choosing this vocation they desire to pass along to other human beings those elements of our culture that will help to enable students to become productive participants in the growth of humanity. Educators live in quest of the truth and passing that truth on to other humans.

Teachers are, then, accountable not only to themselves but to their students and parents and wider community. This is the nature of their work. What parents, students, and community want to know is this: "Tell me the truth, are students learning what they came to you to learn? Tell me the truth, what are their strengths and weaknesses? Tell me the truth, how can they improve?"

A thermometer cannot tell the truth. It is a device that responds to its surroundings as it is designed to do. Humans place marks on its side, set fixed points, divide the distance between those points with marks, place numbers by the marks, and then read the numbers. The numbers only take on meaning when a human tells you what they believe the numbers mean. This is called interpretation. I can tell you that although my wife and I can both see the 77° reading on our thermostat, her experience tells her it is too warm, while mine tells me it is just right. The number does not change, but the interpretation does.

OBLIGATIONS OF ACCOUNTABILITY

Husbands, doctors, parents, teachers, or software engineers are obliged to follow their corresponding ethical standards. Each of us is personally accountable to ourselves, to be a person of our word, and also accountable to those
with whom we are in relationships. Whether our code of ethics is written in
law or within the confines of the profession, we are accountable to those who
hold our promise in trust. I can only do what I have agreed to do. I have free
will and can behave accordingly.

I have no control over the free will of others who may or may not respond
to my actions that are in accordance with my pledge. I just need to have a
clear conscience that I have done what I believed to be appropriate in any
given situation. If I am not as responsive as I should be when my wife is sick,
then she can call me on it. I am accountable to her. If I divulge medical information without patient permission, I am accountable to the patient and
the medical board for a breach of my oath. If I prescribe a treatment method
and/or medication and the patient chooses to ignore it, I am not responsible
for their diminished health.

Accountability says this: "Do what you promised to the best of your ability.
If you are not able to live up to your commitment, then those with whom you
have contracted are free to seek redress from you."

ACCOUNTABILITY THEN AND NOW

Accountability has been with us from the dawn of civilization. From kings to
serfs, from heads of state to citizens, from religious leaders to followers, all are
accountable for their promise to a person or group. In many belief systems, it
is postulated that everyone will eventually be accountable to their god(s) for
how they conducted their lives. So what are we to say about the new "accountability movement" in education? It has bastardized, trivialized, and demeaned
the historical significance and value of genuine accountability. *Educational
accountability is now based on test scores.*

Under the No Child Left Behind Act of 2001 (NCLB), each state is to develop a set of educational standards (see chapter 1). Some states had already
done this prior to NCLB. States were then to develop a set of questions that
are related (they are said to be "aligned") to those standards, contract with
a testing company to make a set of tests containing those questions, and,
finally, give the tests to its students once each year. State boards of education

follow this by arbitrarily selecting a set of cut-off scores that define levels of proficiency for students.

The U.S. Department of Education controls what percentage of students in each school and district should be at this proficiency level. Each year under NCLB, the percentage of students required to be proficient in each school and district is to increase until 100 percent proficiency is achieved in 2014. A state, school district, school, administrator, and teacher have met their accountability mandate if the school has achieved the required percent proficiency. Outside NCLB, many states have their own accountability systems based on similar principles of appropriate test score achievement.

> I argue that just having tests and standards and incentives does not constitute accountability, and in fact, accountability isn't really about how often you test kids and how often you report the results.[2]

TEACHERS' ACCOUNTABILITY BEGINS WITH THEIR PROFESSIONAL STANDARDS

Just like doctors and other professions, each state has its own set of teaching standards or codes of ethics. As an example, here is a summary of California's:

> A developmental view of teaching gives particular attention to the early years of each teacher's career. Beginning teachers move forward in their professional practice in a variety of ways, developing at different rates in different areas of teaching, just as students develop at individual rates in different curricular areas. Support, mentoring, assessment, and advanced study during the early years of teaching are essential to a beginning teacher's development and success in the profession.
>
> Individual teachers enter the profession at varied levels of experience and expertise. The policies and practices of teacher education programs, certification bodies, and school districts must be guided by clear and realistic standards regarding professional performance. The following standards describe best teaching practices at an accomplished level.
>
> Teachers entering the profession with varied levels of prior preparation and competencies will find the standards useful to guide their developing practice as they reflect on their strengths and areas for professional growth in consultation with an experienced support teacher. For these new teachers, the California Standards for the Teaching Profession reflect a developmental view of teaching, and are an integral part of the State's efforts to foster excellence in teaching and learning:

- Engaging and Supporting All Students in Learning
- Creating and Maintaining Effective Environments for Student Learning
- Understanding and Organizing Subject Matter for Student Learning
- Planning Instruction and Designing Learning Experiences for All Students
- Assessing Student Learning
- Developing as a Professional Educator[3]

ACCOUNTABILITY LOST

Educational accountability has lost its fundamental relational nature between humans. It is no longer following through on giving one's word to others. As teachers and administrators, we are bound by our state's teaching standards and/or codes of ethics. Nowhere in NCLB does it state that teachers are being accountable only if they enable their students to produce a specific set of numerical scores and/or percent proficiencies as a result of a once-a-year set of tests.

Teachers, administrators, schools, and districts are accountable to our students every day. This is what professionalism is all about. The "result" that test score accountability seeks is superficial and trivial compared to the impact that each teacher-student interaction has on the educational health and well-being of students.

FACTORS ACCOUNTABILITY CANNOT CONTROL

Educators treat the learning health of their students, just as medical doctors treat students' bodies. Doctors are required to practice following their oath and best procedures and techniques. They can treat, prescribe, and encourage. They cannot *make* a specific percentage of their patients lose weight or lower blood pressure. Patients have the free will to decide to what degree they are willing to follow their physician's prescriptions for health.

Doctors are not responsible for prior health conditions of their patients. Doctors are obliged to practice their medical skills in accordance with their oath and training. Doctors are accountable only for what they can control. This is true whether or not the doctors are in private practice or paid with tax dollars (as most teachers are).

Public school educators are not responsible for the condition of students who are assigned to their classroom. We take whoever shows up at our door. Whatever educational successes and deficiencies they have developed in prior years are not of the teachers' doing. We begin where students are.

The teacher can design and deliver wonderful lessons and require valuable student-appropriate assignments, but this is no guarantee that the student has the skills and the will to follow through. Students have free will. Teachers cannot *make* students learn. They can lead, encourage, and, in some cases, beg. They do this not for the sake of a set of test scores but to help their students become lifelong learners.

ACCOUNTABILITY CORRUPTED

Educators' accountability has been dishonored. Local, state, and national education offices are substituting test score acquisition as the definition of accountability to students, their parents, lawmakers, and the community. The high-stakes testing mantra tries to convince us that a student taking one annual set of multiple-choice tests is the pinnacle of accountability.

This contrivance is directly opposed and contrary to the professional guidelines in educational testing by each state's own educational departments, parent groups, professional educational and psychological organizations, civil rights groups, and some testing companies themselves. Yet this abomination continues.

ACCOUNTABILITY ASSESSED

Should today's teachers, schools, school districts, and states be held accountable? Yes. To whom? Students, parents, and all funding and community agencies that support the educational endeavor. What is their mandate? What are they to promise? Their vow articulated in state laws and written on the hearts of educators is to provide an educational system that encourages and supports lifelong learning available to each and every student.

Through the myriad of grade and course-level descriptions, objectives, and standards, teachers are to apply their skills in the educational process. The entire activity of teachers, administrators, schools, districts, and states is to support lifelong student learning. How will all the stakeholders assess those accountable? How do I assess my doctor's accountability to treat me professionally?

This is done within the context of a doctor's appointment and/or accompanying medical treatment. These are relational questions that are to be answered within the context of our conversations and by experiencing my physician's treatment. These are called formative assessments: assessments that are done as part of the process—not at the end of the process.

STUDENT AND PROFESSIONAL ACCOUNTABILITY

Teachers do this all the time to monitor student accountability. Are students living up to their promise to cooperate in the learning process? Teachers do this in multiple fashions by creating assignments, presentations, projects, quizzes, tests, mastery conferences, portfolios, and the like. They use multiple sources of evidence to determine progress or lack thereof throughout the school year. They report student progress regularly to parents and when necessary meet with them and/or counselors.

A similar accountability process occurs in our schools when trained administrators evaluate teachers within the context of their teaching lessons. Is the instructor following the state's teaching standards (e.g., California's standards noted above)? The administrator consults with the teacher to discuss what went well, what needs to be improved, makes suggestions for doing so, and decides on any consequences for lack of progress. Accountability is also made manifest when administrators are evaluated by district personnel with regard to their job description and so too with school superintendents by the local school board. Each is evaluated within the context of the daily performance of their duties.

Likewise, each school is evaluated by geographic accreditation agencies. For example, the following is the Western Association of Schools and Colleges (WASC) introduction to accreditation:[4]

Why Accreditation?

- Certification to the public that the school is a trustworthy institution of learning
- Validates the integrity of a school's program and student transcripts
- Fosters improvement of the school's programs and operations to support student learning
- Assures a school community that the school's purposes are appropriate and being accomplished through a viable educational program
- A way to manage change through regular assessment, planning, implementing, monitoring and reassessment
- Assists a school/district in establishing its priority areas for improvement as a result of the perpetual accreditation cycle that includes
  - School self-assessment of the current educational program for students
  - Insight and perspective from the visiting committee
  - Regular school staff assessment of progress through the intervening years between full self-studies

A cadre of trained educators meets with each school's staff usually every three to five years and sometimes annually to determine whether the results of their ongoing study in fact conforms to accreditation standards and progress requests. The accountability report is made available to all stakeholders.

INFORMATION-RICH ACCOUNTABILITY

All of this accountability work is already in operation in our schools. Are schools schooling, teachers teaching, and students learning? These are the necessary human interactions that are at the heart of genuine accountability. All stakeholders have access to this information to judge if in fact teachers, administrators, schools, and districts are being accountable to their mandate to provide an educational system designed for students' lifelong learning. Whether students, teachers, administrators, or schools are being evaluated, each accountability process has built within it means for remediation—for the students, teachers, and schools to improve.

TRIANGULATION AND ACCOUNTABILITY

Why, then, is this set of information-rich accountability assessments being trivialized while information-poor high-stakes testing scores loom large and omnipotent? California State professor Art Costa says it quite clearly: "What was once educationally significant, but difficult to measure, has been replaced by what is insignificant and easy to measure. So now we test how well we have taught what we do not value." The current trend in school accountability is to minimize if not substitute the meaning of accountability to the set of test scores and proficiencies that the state and national departments of education require.

There is a term in mathematics called *triangulation*. It is the geometrical process of identifying the location of a point by using angles and distances, the combination of which permits a calculation that uniquely determines the position of the sought-after point. This term is also used in data analysis. It says that if you want to find the most valid truth of a situation, gather quantitative and qualitative information from different perspectives using alternative methods from multiple researchers.

This minimizes research biases by myopic individuals and flawed methods. Scientific studies use triangulation when faced with a new discovery. It requires peers to not only attempt to duplicate the original experiment, but other methods are encouraged to be used across the scientific community to see if they arrive at the same results. In this way, scientists are being accountable to those who finance and benefit from their work. Their accountability mandate is to seek the truth.

When the government requires the use of high-stakes tests, it presents the scores (quantitative data) as a scientifically accurate appraisal of what students know and are able to do. There is no triangulation. There is no verification that this method and its results tell the truth about what a student knows and is able to do. It is taken at face value by the community as a set of judgments about students, teachers, and schools. There are no other sources that validate that these test scores are in fact indicative of student learning.

To whom are the test makers, test administrators, and test interpreters accountable? No one. The fact is that they proclaim their scores and, more importantly, the interpretation of those scores to be the truth because "We said so!" And that is the long and short of it.

NICE VS. MEAN ACCOUNTABILITY

In a 2003 publication, *The Case for Being Mean*, Frederick M. Hess, a resident scholar at American Enterprise Institute (AEI), writes:

> Simply put, there are two kinds of accountability: suggestive and coercive, or, more plainly, "nice" and "mean." Advocates of nice accountability presume that the key to school improvement is to provide educators with more resources, expertise, training, support, and "capacity." They view accountability as a helpful tool that seeks to improve schooling by developing standards, applying informal social pressures, using tests as a diagnostic device increasing coordination across schools and classrooms, and making more efficient use of school resources through standardization. The educational benefits produced by nice accountability depend on individual volition.
>
> Mean accountability, on the other hand, uses coercive measures—incentives and sanctions—to ensure that educators teach and students master specific content. Students must demonstrate their mastery of essential knowledge and skills in the areas of math, writing, reading, and perhaps core disciplines at certain key points and before graduating from high school. Educators are expected to do what is necessary to ensure that they no longer pass on students unequipped for the most fundamental requirements of further education, work, or good citizenship.
>
> In such a system, school performance no longer rests on fond wishes and good intentions. Instead, such levers as diplomas and job security are used to

compel students and teachers to cooperate. Mean accountability seeks to harness the self-interest of students and educators to refocus schools and redefine the expectations of teachers and learners.[5]

AEI is a business-oriented conservative think tank. Its motto is "Competition of ideas is fundamental to a free society."

NO FREEDOM IN MEAN ACCOUNTABILITY

It is interesting to note that while Hess (AEI) values a free society, he does not value freedom in education, but rather coercion. He advocates force to compel students and teachers to cooperate with the high-stakes testing regime. I really admire the honesty but not the substance of his thinking. It sounds like it could easily be the educational manifesto of a totalitarian regime.

He clearly defines a mindset that is at the heart of high-stakes scores in his "mean" accountability. Its focus is only on numerical output. I interpret this to mean that there is little care for what goes on in the classroom. The hows and whys are not important. But what is important are the resulting numbers. Mean accountability means that the only significant outcome is a set of high-stakes test scores and how they can be used to judge teachers, schools, and districts, and force change.

How do those who agree with "mean" accountability apply this concept to those who are in favor of the use of high-stakes testing? They don't. Many in the business community interpret the high-stakes test results from local, state, and national students' testing without themselves having any accountability. Who is permitted to stand in opposition to their inferences? Any comments made contrary to their conclusions are deemed "sour grapes," or just an excuse to "mitigate the obvious." There is no court of last resort. This is tantamount to a legal case where the prosecutor presents one bit of evidence, none is allowed by the defense, and guilt the only permitted outcome.

OPPRESSION AND POWER

What is the evolution of this kind of thinking and sentiment? How does it eventually impact the freedom of students to express themselves as unique individuals? How does it utilize fear and threats to keep everyone in line? Mean accountability is nothing more than a strategy to coerce students and teachers to do the bidding of those who consider themselves powerful.

[Eli] Broad, founder of two Fortune 500 companies, was the 39th richest person in America last year, according to Forbes magazine. And he is very interested in putting a good chunk of his billions into K–12 public education. He says urban public schools are failing and must adopt methods from business to succeed, such as competition, accountability based on "measurables," and unhampered management authority—all focusing on the bottom line of student achievement, as measured by standardized tests. Broad wants to create competition by starting publicly funded, privately run charter schools, to enforce accountability by linking teacher pay to student test scores, and to limit teachers' say in curriculum and transfer decisions.[6]

Those who espouse mean accountability say, "Produce this or else!" It is an irrational disregard for freedom; as such, it becomes a form of systemic evil. This has nothing to do with whether or not they believe that these scores are telling the truth about what a student knows and is able to do. It has all to do with having found a method of control to manipulate public education. Students and educators must do their bidding.

Mean accountability creates a set of numerical mandates intended to forcibly control schools by pressuring educational administrators to pressure its teachers, so that teachers can in turn pressure their students. It is hoped that in this manner, from a very young age, students will be trained to understand that whoever controls the numbers controls their lives. The numbers begin as high-stakes test scores and end up as wages, salaries, worker benefits, and the like.

The current accountability fad insists on mandates that are not only overly detailed but chosen according to whether they lend themselves to easy measurement. It's not just that the tests are supposed to be tied to the standards; it's that the standards have been selected on the basis of their testability. The phrase "specific, measurable standards" suggests a commitment not to excellence but to behaviorism.

It is telling that this phrase is heard most often from corporate officials and politicians, not from leading educational theorists or cognitive scientists. . . . Concepts like intrinsic motivation and intellectual exploration are difficult for some minds to grasp, whereas test scores, like sales figures or votes, can be calculated and charted and used to define success and failure.[7]

TOTALITARIAN ACCOUNTABILITY

"Mean" accountability is defined by those who fear losing what they consider their superior position in our society. From the outset, NCLB was founded on "mean" accountability, intending to "whip into shape" students, teachers, schools, districts, and states. Susan Neuman, an assistant secretary of education during the early years of NCLB, exposed the transition from what was considered the "nice" accountability of the Clinton administration to those espousing "mean" accountability:

> Tensions between NCLB believers and the blow-up-the-schools group were one reason the Bush Department of Education felt like "a pressure cooker," says Neuman, who left the Administration in early 2003. Another reason was political pressure to take the hardest possible line on school accountability in order to avoid looking lax—like the Clinton administration.
>
> Thus, when Neuman and others argued that many schools would fail to reach the NCLB goals and needed more flexibility while making improvements, they were ignored. "We had this no-waiver policy," says Neuman. "The feeling was that the prior administration had given waivers willy-nilly."[8]

So we are really down to this: Genuine accountability has become corrupted. What once was the pride of teachers' personal commitment to their students in all of its complexity and attention to each as an individual has become narrowed and minimized to a set of numerical scores that cannot tell the truth about what a student knows and is able to do.

What is even worse is that, in the name of accountability, students' importance to their teachers and school is reduced as they are viewed as score producers. This demeans their personal value to themselves and society. The fallout is that oftentimes teachers and parents become the drivers who encourage and reinforce this mentality.

> Thus teachers end up in ridiculous binds, the students and the teachers suffer from destructive approaches to "accountability," deep social problems remain unaddressed as schools take the fall for society, test makers and prep companies make money, many politicians pat themselves on the back for having done something, and many business people talk about making better schools when corporate-promoted schemes are making schools worse for the people in them.[9]

5

Is Education for Profit?

Here's how Merrill Lynch described the corporate offensive in their April 9, 1999, report called *The Book of Knowledge: Investing in the Growing Education and Training Industry*:

> A new mindset is necessary, one that views families as customers, schools as retail outlets where educational services are received, and the school board as a customer service department that hears and address parental concerns.[1]

Lehman Brothers managing director, Mary Tanner, stated at their first conference on privatization in 1996:

> Education today, like health care 30 years ago, is a vast, highly localized industry ripe for change. The emergence of HMOs and hospital management companies created enormous opportunities for investors. We believe the same pattern will occur in education.[2]

Fredrick Hess, editor of *Educational Entrepreneurship: Realities, Challenges, Possibilities*, makes the designs on schools quite clear:

> There are steps that would make K–12 schooling more attractive to for-profit investment, triggering a significant infusion of money to support research, development, and creative problem-solving. For one, imposing clear standards for judging educational effectiveness would reassure investors that ventures will

be less subject to political brickbats and better positioned to succeed if demonstrably effective. A more performance-based environment enables investors to assess risk in a more informed, rational manner.[3]

Big business has its eye on education. It's a wide-open field for investment and a possible lucrative source of income. If it can be demonstrated that public schools are failing, then there would be the possibility of offering a better product for the public to buy. The corporate world would have to redefine the goals of schools to fit what it has to offer.

Motives for America to educate its youth have changed over the past 230 years. In seventeenth-century New England, the deep Puritanical-Calvinistic zeal for learning was a bulwark of church and state. For the colonial Protestants, the aim of school was religion, morality, and knowledge—all being necessary for good government and the happiness of the community.

The focus was on the individual and their personal betterment. The cultural norm was simple enough. Help develop good people and you will have a good society. Newly won freedoms were translated into the academic freedoms to do what you will with your education. With the industrial revolution of the nineteenth century, we see a gradual shift of this paradigm.

INDUSTRY NEEDS EDUCATED WORKERS

Industry needed literate and competent workers to manufacture products that would be competitive in the marketplace. It is no wonder, then, that in the latter part of the nineteenth century we began to see a radical increase in the number of states enacting compulsory education laws. Industry needs individuals who can read, write, and work with numbers.

What does becoming an industrial worker offer? The opportunity to make more money by working more with your brain than with your brawn, as was necessary on the farms. Industry wants to hire the very best, and so it begins to put demands on the educational system to provide information as to the quality of its students. Education is becoming less and less for personal growth, but rather to satisfy business needs.

JUSTICE AND CIVIL RIGHTS MOVEMENTS

The 1960s and 1970s were revolutionary in many ways. Those most marginalized in America began to seek redress, if not peacefully, in any way that those in power would have to hear: the civil rights movement, women's liberation, student and black power, the Watts riots, anti-Vietnam war demonstrations.

All screamed out for justice. Though apparently separate movements, they gained energy from each other in trying to wrest control of our country from those who had come to be captains of the American ship. Indeed, there was a mutiny of sorts. There is a line of thinking that supports the notion that the assassinations of President John F. Kennedy, Martin Luther King, and Attorney General Robert Kennedy were reactions to the hope that the oppressed members of our country were actually going to have powerful advocates in leadership positions.

Old thinking and prejudices were challenged. The hippie counterculture movement rejected established institutions, criticized middle-class values, opposed nuclear weapons and war, embraced aspects of Eastern religions, championed a sexual revolution of free love, and promoted the use of drugs to expand one's consciousness.

EDUCATION'S WAR ON POVERTY

Those marginalized began to make both political and economic strides. In education, President Lyndon B. Johnson's war on poverty (circa 1964) inaugurated the Elementary and Secondary Education Act (ESEA—now modified to become NCLB, No Child Left Behind), which was to augment local education finances with federal funds for primary and secondary education.

As mandated in the act, the funds were authorized for educators' professional development, instructional materials, resources to support educational programs, and parental involvement. Along with that, the Head Start program was initiated to provide comprehensive school readiness education, health, nutrition, and parent involvement services to low-income children and their families.

EDUCATION FAULTED

In 1957, the Soviet Union successfully launched Sputnik, the first man-made satellite to circle Earth. The seeds of anxiety began. How could this have happened? How about America's future? It was thought that our educational system must be at fault. A massive influx of funds for math and science education entered U.S. schools. Suffice it to say that the Russians and Americans both commandeered German rocket scientists after World War II. The German scientists whom the Russians sequestered under their control were more successful than ours. But blame was put squarely on our schools. Why?

Whose fault is it when in football a kicker misses the winning field goal with just a few seconds to play? Is it really the kicker? How about the two interceptions in the first quarter? Or the lineman that missed a block that led to a two-point safety in the second quarter, or the quarterback's interception returned for a touchdown in the third? Who is the easiest scapegoat? Who is least able to defend themselves—the kicker or the quarterback? Do you think that the industrial-military complex will admit it was their failure? (NASA did not come into existence until after Sputnik.) Or do you think that it was easier to blame schools?

TOTAL QUALITY MANAGEMENT

Meanwhile, on the economic front after World War II, the Marshall Plan was enabling Europe to get back on its feet as we also gave much support to the recovery of Japan. In the early 1950s, Dr. W. Edwards Deming was hired by the post-war government of Japan to help with their census. In the process he introduced their manufacturing leaders to a program called total quality management (TQM). It contained fourteen points:

1. Create constancy of purpose for improvement of product and service. Constancy of purpose requires innovation, investment in research and education, continuous improvement of product and service, maintenance of equipment, furniture and fixtures, and new aids to production.
2. Adopt the new philosophy. Management must undergo a transformation and begin to believe in quality products and services.
3. Cease dependence on mass inspection. Inspect products and services only enough to be able to identify ways to improve the process.
4. End the practice of awarding business on price tag alone. The lowest-priced goods are not always the highest quality; choose a supplier based on its record of improvement and then make a long-term commitment to it.
5. Improve constantly and forever the system of product and service. Improvement is not a one-time effort; management is responsible for leading the organization into the practice of continual improvement in quality and productivity.

6. Institute training and retraining. Workers need to know how to do their jobs correctly even if they need to learn new skills.

7. Institute leadership. Leadership is the job of management. Managers have the responsibility to discover the barriers that prevent staff from taking pride in what they do. The staff will know what those barriers are.

8. Drive out fear. People often fear reprisal if they "make waves" at work. Managers need to create an environment where workers can express concerns with confidence.

9. Break down barriers between staff areas. Managers should promote teamwork by helping staff in different areas/departments work together. Fostering interrelationships among departments encourages higher quality decision-making.

10. Eliminate slogans, exhortations, and targets for the workforce. Using slogans alone, without an investigation into the processes of the workplace, can be offensive to workers because they imply that a better job could be done. Managers need to learn real ways of motivating people in their organizations.

11. Eliminate numerical quotas. Quotas impede quality more than any other working condition; they leave no room for improvement. Workers need the flexibility to give customers the level of service they need.

12. Remove barriers to pride of workmanship. Give workers respect and feedback about how they are doing their jobs.

13. Institute a vigorous program of education and retraining. With continuous improvement, job descriptions will change. As a result, employees need to be educated and retrained so they will be successful at new job responsibilities.

14. Take action to accomplish the transformation. Management must work as a team to carry out the previous thirteen steps.

The message is to focus more on the *process* of developing a quality product rather than the rate of production. That process involves respecting the *input* of the workers to produce the product in a harmonious way. Over the next thirty years, as Japan began to embed TQM into its manufacturing infrastructure, it experienced dramatic economic growth. Deming returned to the United States and was unknown for years until the publication of his book *Out of the Crisis* in 1982. He believed that if American manufacturers followed this model they would be able to avoid the fate of being behind the Japanese.

U.S. BUSINESS CHALLENGED

In the 1980s, when the United States began to see a reduction in its own world market share in relation to Japan, American business rediscovered Deming. But in doing so they "translated" Deming's fourteen points in such a way as to define quality more rigidly in terms of its ability to be measured in a reproducible fashion based on a given standard output.

This assumed that all the raw materials are themselves provided at a given standard with little variation so that you have a high probability of processing this raw material and producing the desired product. In this way you do not have to test every item made for quality but sample the products. For example, if every fifth product fits the standard, then that would be sufficient. No need to test the others.

EDUCATION AGAIN A SCAPEGOAT

Gradually, our corporate world was beginning to be more and more challenged by foreign businesses. Do you think it was incumbent on the corporate and government communities to examine their policies and practices to see how they were being outsmarted by these upstarts in the race for the dollar? The corporate world cried out, "Oh, my God, how could we be losing our financial hold on the rest of the world? It must be fallout from all the free thinking of the 1960s and 1970s!" Instead of investigating the weaknesses and fallacies that drove their own business practices, they diverted public attention by using our education system as a scapegoat.

> It's not the job of teachers to make students more competitive with the Chinese given that such competition serves the interests of corporations, not the larger interests of U.S. society. As David Stratman argues, "Beginning with *A Nation at Risk*, nearly all of the education reform plans have been couched in terms of one great national purpose: business competition. According to these plans, the great goal and measure of national and educational progress is how effectively U.S. corporations compete with Japanese and German corporations in the international marketplace. I think that most educators—most people, in fact—are downright uncomfortable with the idea that the fulfillment of our hu-

man potential is best measured by the Gross National Product or the progress of Microsoft or General Motors stock on the Big Board."[4]

A NATION AT RISK

The publication of *A Nation at Risk* in 1983 initiated the corporate and governmental cry for accountability in education. It began with the following:

> Our Nation is at risk. Our once unchallenged preeminence in commerce, industry, science, and technological innovation is being overtaken by competitors throughout the world. This report is concerned with only one of the many causes and dimensions of the problem, but it is the one that under girds American prosperity, security, and civility.
>
> We report to the American people that while we can take justifiable pride in what our schools and colleges have historically accomplished and contributed to the United States and the well-being of its people, the educational foundations of our society are presently being eroded by a rising tide of mediocrity that threatens our very future as a Nation and a people. What was unimaginable a generation ago has begun to occur—others are matching and surpassing our educational attainments.
>
> We live among determined, well-educated, and strongly motivated competitors. We compete with them for international standing and markets, not only with products but also with the ideas of our laboratories and neighborhood workshops. America's position in the world may once have been reasonably secure with only a few exceptionally well-trained men and women. It is no longer. . . . If only to keep and improve on the slim competitive edge we still retain in world markets, we must dedicate ourselves to the reform of our educational system for the benefit of all—old and young alike, affluent and poor, majority and minority.

The report concluded,

> It is by our willingness to take up the challenge, and our resolve to see it through, that America's place in the world will be either secured or forfeited.[5]

SKINNER AND BLOOM

Coupled with this was the evolving educational psychology of the prolific B. F. Skinner (1904–1990), who proposed a method of using rewards and lack of rewards (punishments) to stimulate students to attain mastery of concepts. This was called behavior modification. These ideas melded with the work of Professor Benjamin Bloom (1913–1999), who is known as the father of outcome-based education (OBE), or, more recently, "standards-based education."

This combination made for the formulation in the 1980s and 1990s of an educational system that encouraged the use of selected rewards and punishments to attain mastery of standards such as those explained in chapter 1.

> The current delivery systems in New Zealand are driven by and structured within business models and business ideas such as efficiency and effectiveness. These ideas have displaced educational theory and philosophy as the articulated main focus of education, but are these business concepts enough? I suggest to view education as confined to these concepts is to make the mistake of measuring only outcomes and ignoring process and essence.
>
> Education is bigger than these concepts. Thomas Merton (circa 1967) suggested "we are warmed by fire not by the smoke of the fire. We are carried over the sea by a ship not by the wake of a ship." So we should be careful we are not distracted through measuring the smoke, or gauging the wake or judging the froth but have chosen carefully what we consider really matters.[6]

THE GENESIS OF HIGH-STAKES TESTING

So here is a recap of how accountability (the corporate business version applied to schools) came to be redefined in terms of appropriate scores resulting from high-stakes testing:

- Following World War II, both Europe and Japan began to improve their economic status in the world in part through American programs designed to bring them back from the destruction of the war.
- In 1950s Japan, American Edwards Deming's total quality management (TQM) manufacturing program focused on improving quality through process *inputs*, igniting Japan's economy.
- In 1957, the Soviet Union launched Sputnik, and the military-industrial complex blamed our educational system rather than their own policies and practices.
- In the turbulent 1960s and 1970s, assassinations of American leaders who empathized with the poor and disenfranchised, as well as riots and war protests, spawned a cultural and educational revolution. This riled corporate America.
- In order to bring more resources to bear, Lyndon Johnson's war on poverty (1964) inaugurated the Elementary and Secondary Education Act

(ESEA—modified in 2001 to become NCLB, No Child Left Behind), which was to augment local education finances with federal funds for primary and secondary education, as well as the Head Start program for the poor. Focus was on inputs: money and resources.

- In the early 1980s, as corporate America began to lose more of its share of the market to Japan and rising European companies, U.S. manufacturers discovered Deming and began to utilize major elements of TQM—especially comparing a product to given measurable standards in order to produce quality products. This meshed with the corporate drive to improve production outputs.
- *A Nation at Risk* (1983) concluded that America was losing its competitive edge and the reason was a lax educational system. No responsibility was placed on corporate and government business policies. Fear of profit loss was the driving force.
- Throughout the 1980s and 1990s, the work of B. F. Skinner meshed with that of Benjamin Bloom and initiated the use of outcome-based education (OBE)—teaching to a set of content standards, parallel to Deming's product standards.
- Three hundred CEOs met in 1989 and agreed that each state needed to adopt legislation that would impose "outcome-based education," "high expectations for all children," and "rewards and penalties for individual schools." They essentially applied OBE and their version of TQM, which was focused on measurable outcomes, not process.
- The measurable outcomes utilized would be standardized test scores given in a primarily multiple-choice format once each academic year. This is their version of TQM applied to schools. Accountability then is determined by arbitrary selection of cut scores and proficiency percentages.

This whole history became codified in the high-stakes testing principle with its coercive "mean" accountability (see chapter 4) that underpins the No Child Left Behind Act of 2001. Noted education historian Dr. Kathy Emery elucidated this as part of a panel presentation at the San Francisco State University Faculty retreat at Asilomar, California, on January 26, 2005:

> No Child Left Behind represents only the latest manifestation of a bipartisan bandwagon of "standards based advocates"—a bandwagon built in the summer of 1989 by the top 300 CEOs in our country. At this meeting, the Business Roundtable CEOs agreed that each state legislature needed to adopt legislation

that would impose "outcome-based education," "high expectations for all children," "rewards and penalties for individual schools," "greater school-based decision making" and align staff development with these action items.

By 1995, the Business Roundtable had refined their agenda to "nine essential components," the first four being state standards, state tests, sanctions, and the transformation of teacher education programs. By 2000, our leading CEOs had managed to create an interlocking network of business associations, corporate foundations, governors' associations, nonprofits, and educational institutions that had successfully persuaded 16 state legislatures to adopt the first three components of their high-stakes testing agenda.[7]

HUMAN CAPITAL AND COMPETITION

Schools are accused of being the institutions that have not provided the quality "human capital"—that is, capable enough students required to make corporate America more "competitive" (i.e., we will make more profit and have a larger share of the market than other like businesses).

Both the National Alliance for Business and, more strongly, the Business Roundtable continue to use their power and influence to lobby state and federal legislators to use a competition-oriented, data-driven model of rewards and punishments to administrate public schools. Their premise is that improving high-stakes test scores will result in a more "competitive" America. The fact is that this is not true:

> American students don't score at the top of the class in math and science compared with students from other industrialized countries. They're average, and sometimes below average. Does that matter? Not a bit, says Keith Baker, a former U.S. Education Department analyst, and he says he can prove it. In an article due to be published later this year, Baker looks at how well math scores predict the performance of a nation's economy.
>
> The answer: They don't. Baker's analysis begins with the scores of the 12-year-olds from 11 industrialized nations who took part in the First International Math Study (FIMS) in 1964. American students came in second to last, ahead of only Sweden. Baker looked at what happened decades later when those 12-year-olds were running the U.S. economy. America's economy grew at a rate of 3.3 percent per year from 1992 to 2002. The countries that scored higher than the U.S. grew at a slower rate—2.5 percent—during the same period.

All in all, countries that did better in the test competition did worse in the economic competition. Did the higher scores result in more innovation—which might show up in the number of patents? No again. The United States "clobbered the world on creativity, with 326 patents per million people," compared with 127 per million in the countries whose kids scored higher, Baker reports.[8]

COMPETITION, COMPETITION, COMPETITION

Still, the corporate mantra continues, "We need to strive for higher test scores so that students can be successful in the globally competitive marketplace, and if they are successful, so are we." What will it take to convince legislative decision-makers that this myth is nothing more than business disinformation?

Which leads to the third—and very widely accepted—myth: that *international test-score comparisons are valid measures of a country's ability to compete in the global economy* [emphasis in original]. The fact that we can't interpret these test-score comparisons has not deterred us from concluding that a country's international competitiveness can be predicted from its ranking on international tests. There is a long history of drawing that inference. The early international comparisons, conducted shortly after the launch of Sputnik in 1957, reinforced our fear that the Soviet Union was overtaking us in science and technology.

Later, Japan was the country to fear because of its trade balance and its industrial-management techniques. Now, we are most concerned about China and India, two countries with rapid growth that have made large gains in technical fields. In each case, a concern about other countries' accomplishments became linked in our minds with a concern about the ranking of U.S. students on international test-score comparisons.[9]

Just where are we in the world regarding our "competitive" edge? If being competitive really is important to some, then what has happened immediately prior to the inception of the testing mania (circa 2001 and the No Child Left Behind Act)? Our competitive status should show us what needs to be done in schools—assuming that education *is* the key to greater profits.

Remember that the standards and high-stakes testing era began in the late 1990s. This means that in order to see its most positive effect we can begin with kindergarteners in 1997. They have had twelve years of this type of learning and, upon completing twelve years of public school education, graduated in 2009. Depending on years of post–high school education, productivity in the business sector, for those who enter it, will not occur until after 2010. So that right now, according to the 1983 publication of *A Nation at Risk*, we should see that our competitive edge has been slipping away over the past twenty-seven years.

> You guys don't seem to get it. *A Nation at Risk* (ANAR) said we were doomed if we didn't completely reform our schools. You point out that today we're #25 among 30 industrialized nations in math. So we didn't shape up as ANAR demanded. Yet the World Economic Forum ranks us the most competitive economy in the world. So does the Institute for Management Development. The IMD had us replacing Japan as #1 in 1994 and remaining in that position. You remember Japan. It had a great economy, and the people who wrote ANAR thought that that was due to Japanese kids' high test scores.
>
> After ANAR appeared, Secretary of Education Ted Bell dispatched Assistant Secretary Checker Finn and a group of policy wonks to Japan to see if we could import their schools. They said they thought it was possible. But 7 years later, Japan's economy sank into the Pacific and took the rest of the Asian Tiger nations with it. But Japanese kids continued to ace tests. Get it through your head: tests don't count.[10]

What do our Chinese "competitors" have to say about our educational system?

> "Global competitiveness depends on students' abilities to innovate and invent, not on their test scores," agrees Yong Zhao, professor and director of the U.S.-China Center for Research on Educational Excellence at Michigan State University. America has long embraced its students' passion, ingenuity, dreams, and ideas—none of which can be measured by test scores, says Zhao. Asia, on the other hand, has traditionally valued test scores above all else.
>
> Even where scores are high and innovative educational approaches are valued, as in Singapore, it's still felt that testing plays too much of a role. "Yours is a talent meritocracy, ours is an exam meritocracy," Tharman Shanmugaratnam, Minister of Education of Singapore, said in a *Newsweek* interview. "There are some parts of the intellect that we are not able to test well—like creativity, curiosity, a sense of adventure, ambition. . . . America has a culture of learning that challenges conventional wisdom, even if it means challenging authority. These are the areas where Singapore must learn from America." But the increased focus on standardized testing here threatens to push American education in the wrong direction, experts warn. "We're reducing our ability to be competitive

with measures like NCLB," Zhao says. "We're disadvantaging our students by celebrating points and test scores rather than what really matters."[11]

And yet more evidence of the test-score-competition myth:

Political leaders, tech executives, and academics often claim that the U.S. is falling behind in math and science education. They cite poor test results, declining international rankings, and decreasing enrollment in the hard sciences. They urge us to improve our education system and to graduate more engineers and scientists to keep pace with countries such as India and China. Yet a *new report* by the Urban Institute, a nonpartisan think tank, tells a different story [emphasis in original]. . . .

The authors of the report, the Urban Institute's Hal Salzman and Georgetown University professor Lindsay Lowell, show that math, science, and reading test scores at the primary and secondary level have increased over the past two decades, and U.S. students are now close to the top of international rankings. Perhaps just as surprising, the report finds that our education system actually produces more science and engineering graduates than the market demands.[12]

And finally, what does the international business community say about the status of America's "competitiveness"?

The United States is assessed this year as the world's most competitive economy; endowed with a combination of sophisticated and innovative companies operating in very efficient factor markets. This is buttressed by an excellent university system and strong collaboration between the educational and business sectors in research and development.[13]

Table 5.1.   Rankings 2007–2008 Top Ten

Rank	Country	Score
1	United States	5.67
2	Switzerland	5.62
3	Denmark	5.55
4	Sweden	5.54
5	Germany	5.51
6	Finland	5.49
7	Singapore	5.45
8	Japan	5.43
9	United Kingdom	5.41
10	Netherlands	5.40

So enough of this forced Business Roundtable's causal link between test scores and competitiveness. It does not exist. But what does exist now is a system so focused on raising test scores that it suppresses students' freedom to think creatively and develop a lifelong desire to learn.

DIFFERENT GOALS, DIFFERENT PROCESSES

The goal of business is to make a profit for the owners and employees. The goal of marriage is the satisfaction and joy of a shared life. The goal of our educational system is to enable our students to be lifelong learners in whatever path they choose in life so that they can contribute meaningfully to our society. The goal of government is to oversee, protect, and nurture the well-being of the citizens it serves.

Just as business, marriage, education, and government have different goals, they also have different processes that lead to those goals. Business uses people in relationships to operate, but this does not make it a marriage. And, conversely, just because a marriage uses money to operate does not make it a business. Relationships and finances are parts of marriages, businesses, religious groups, and governments. Each has different goals and employs processes consistent with them. Should businesses be full of couple love because successful marriages are? Should marriages then unite and use their power to assure that all businesses are run by married couples?

Married couples pay taxes to run governments. Should government employees therefore be required to love one another? Although individuals may view any enterprise as a means to a profit, this does not mean that all organizations, whether public or private, should have profit as their goal.

MUTUAL RESPECT

We are mutually interdependent, but that does not and should not make us all operate under the same paradigm. What will benefit each organization is the liberty it has to develop its own identity under law, and then possibly use that autonomy to freely choose to be in relationship with other entities. Business and education have cooperated on a number of fronts for many years. The times in which educators observe business profits faltering should not be an opportunity to lobby legislators to insist all business personnel go back to school. Nor should the government save failing businesses for their own sake, but rather for the sake of the greater good.

Should then CEOs and attendant executives be elected on the basis of a democratic voting by employees? Our interdependence does not give permission to governments to take over marriages or businesses to take over schools. The desire for profit does not trump the desire for academic freedom. Forcing all business to be run by married couples would be just as disastrous as forcing all schools to be run by business interests.

What is needed is mutual respect. Each group needs to respect the gifts and talents that the other has invested in their enterprise of choice. Education enterprises should value what married couples, government, and business bring to the community.

STAY OUT OF EACH OTHER'S "BUSINESS"

Business should respect and support education. Education should listen to the needs of business, as it should the needs of government and society as a whole. Any attempt to usurp education's autonomy and authority to make decisions regarding the education of youth is a serious breach of trust. It is an insult and should be confronted as we do in this work.

Public schools are not an organ of corporate America. They do not exist to provide the "human capital" for its ongoing operations. Corporate America has made its intent quite clear in this matter. Many corporations will go to other countries (called outsourcing) to manufacture and develop its products if it can make a greater profit. In the vast majority of cases, this outsourcing is not based on the unavailability of qualified workers here in America—it is "good business sense" to go where costs are less and profits are greater.

Public schools exist to serve students at the behest of their parents and are funded by government. Schools do not exist to support corporate profits and nurture economic global competition. That is the business of business. Schools educate so that students will have the freedom to choose their path in life. Maybe they want to be social workers, teachers, nurses, or ministers in a religious setting. Maybe they do not want to buy into being competitive.

I was presenting standardized test scores to a group of parents when I unconsciously parroted an often-heard phrase, "In order to be economically competitive in the 21st century, we have to have high test scores." A mother's hand shot up, "But I don't want my son to be an international competitor in a 21st century global economy," she declared. "I want him to be a good man." The room fell silent. She went on, "I want him to hold a good job, carry his own weight, and give a little bit more to his community than he took. I want him to get along with others. I want him to love and be loved. I want him to be happy." With stunning and simple eloquence, this mother brilliantly defined the purposes of education.[14]

Not only parents but teachers also are asked to cast their lot in with the competitive business model of education. Teachers are being enlisted to be the school site instruments of competition and indoctrination of students. This conflicts directly with teachers' desire to teach cooperation and collaboration, hallmarks of growth and progress in any civilization.

> But I have to start with the question: Do I as an educator want to enlist in this war? Who recruited me to do battle with the workers of India, or China, or Brazil? Somehow, all the administrators and teachers in America are supposed to sign up for this economic war. We want to beat the foreigners down. We want to keep our position as less than five percent of the world's population consuming 60 percent of the world's resources.
>
> But a teacher may reply, "No, thank you." I don't really have anything against the Indian, the Chinese, the Mexican, or other workers. Of course, if I knew the bloke personally, or his or her family, I'd want them to do very well. If I were asked to look that person in the eye over a large table of food, and to clear away most of the food for my family, leaving him or her with just a pittance, would I jump at the chance? No.
>
> But we are asked to gamely sign up for this competition—in order to keep our position way, way out ahead of others in terms of consumption. I respectfully decline. And ultimately the only road to peace in this world is for that gap, that income differential, that inequitable distribution of resources, dignity, power, freedom to narrow over the next hundred years.[15]

SCHOOLS ARE NOT MANUFACTURING PLANTS

Big business wants to limit the choices that students have to those that are of benefit to its operations. It wants schools to be manufacturing plants that produce students to its specifications. It wants to limit academic freedom and enforce a one-size-fits-all mentality that is rooted in creating an obedient and, when possible, a low-wage worker to enhance profits. A teacher, Steve Strauss, has this to say about the interplay between business and education:

> "Competition in the international marketplace is, in reality, a battle for the classroom." With this 1993 salvo, the Business Roundtable, an association of

about 150 CEOs from the nation's most powerful corporations, announced its intention to occupy U.S. public schools. The goal? To turn public schools into "workforce development systems," an assembly line model of schooling designed to manufacture a new U.S. labor force that would ensure corporate America's competitive edge over European and Asian rivals.

In an insulting move to "teacher-proof" the classroom, many teachers are now forced to use scripted lesson plans. They literally recite prepared lines, await the kids' responses, and move to the next line.[16]

A parent, Scott W. Baker, weighs in on what he does not want for his daughters:

Here, in a nutshell, is what has happened: In 1989 the national Business Roundtable decided that Total Quality Management (a production model aimed at eliminating waste and producing high-quality products) would work as well when applied to the education of humans as it did when applied to the manufacture of toasters/cars, etc. The resulting reform goals were marketed as "Outcomes-Based Education." Outcomes became standards and benchmarks. A child is not a toaster. My daughters are presently nobody's human capital![17]

With the merging of TQM and OBE, mean accountability (chapter 4) found two processes under the mantle of NCLB that were easily utilized as tools to undermine American education. Under the banner word of *accountability*, the state and federal governments have cooperated with the mindset of the Business Roundtable to create an education system that will mold citizens into ineffective, fearful, and mindless peons who will do as they are directed, never question what they are told, and forget about what true intellectual freedom without boundaries ever felt like.

There are real engineering (never mind ethical) problems in applying a manufacturing model to human beings. In manufacturing you are attempting to apply uniform processes to uniform materials to achieve uniform results. In manufacturing you have a clear specification of desired performance and unambiguous, precise, and easily applied measures of compliance. In manufacturing you weed out and eliminate defective materials and parts as early in the process as possible. . . .

In our educational "factories" we do not start with uniform materials nor do we expect or is it even desirable to achieve uniform results. In education we cannot weed out and eliminate defective parts. None of the assumptions above apply. Yet we are imposing a framework intended for manufacturing on the schools and pretending it works. Being good little workers, the school administrators and their employees are doing what they're told: improve the statistics. . . .

Statistics do not go out and hold jobs and have families and vote and make decisions and all the other things that real human beings do. Surely that student at rank 45 is just as much a real human being as the student at rank 59, but because he is less likely to contribute to improving the class statistics he is treated as less of one. All the players in this completely whacked out system believe they are doing their jobs. Thus, the school systems are shameless about trying to manipulate the curve because they think that's what they are supposed to do and I guess it is! I feel like Charlton Heston in Planet of the Apes: "This is a mad house!"[18]

IS THIS WHAT WE WANT FOR OUR CHILDREN?

Now is the time. Enough of the Business Roundtable's attacks on public school education. We friends of education must move on the offensive to demonstrate by businesses' own numerical standards how their frustrated quest for adequate profits is, by and large, a result of their own poor business practices and governmental policies, and not poor high-stakes test scores.

American economic competitiveness with Japan and other nations is to a considerable degree a function of monetary, trade, and industrial policy, and of decisions made by the President and Congress, the Federal Reserve Board, and the Federal Departments of the Treasury, Commerce, and Labor.

Therefore, to conclude that problems of international competitiveness can be solved by educational reform, especially educational reform defined solely as school reform, is not merely utopian and millennialist, it is at best a foolish and at worst a crass effort to direct attention away from those truly responsible for doing something about competitiveness and to lay the burden instead on the schools. It is a device that has been used repeatedly in the history of American education.[19]

Now is the time to reveal how their failed practices and policies are costing Americans jobs and some measure of financial security and are bankrupting large and small businesses, not to mention education. In the quest for excessive profits, white-collar crime is costing innocent workers and investors their future.

BIG BUSINESS NEEDS TO BE PUT IN ITS PLACE

Now is the time for the Business Roundtables to look into the mirror and take the log out of their eyes rather than continually attempting to take the speck out of education's eye. They wait for student test scores in hopes of validating their twisted perspectives on education. And all the while, we have an entire economy whose financial decline is obvious even to the blind.

What cause is there to excuse *their* financial folly? Can we say that the market is cyclical and use this as a reason to tolerate their foolishness? Can we demand that business leaders cloister themselves until they admit the error of their ways and redirect their efforts for the benefit of all? Or is there a more sinister and self-serving side to their "concern" for education?

> The argument in this book [*Marketing Fear in America's Public Schools*] is that the short answer is money. And, the long answer is money, both the money that corporations stand to make off their scripted, supposedly scientifically based, prepackaged programs and the money schools stand to lose in terms of decreased federal funding if they do not use such programs. Education is the last major public institution in the United States that is not primarily in the hands of corporate control.
>
> Public education represents a multibillion-dollar opportunity to private enterprise. By creating the myth of failure of teachers and colleges of education, the political, conservative, and corporate right can then of course institute privatization.[20]

Business needs to be put in its place. Big business is not the panacea for the world's problems, let alone education. As long as we use language like "the school plant" and "building committee," and treat superintendents as if they are CEOs and schools like they are big businesses, we will lose the uniqueness of a professional educator's interacting with students for the students' hopes, dreams, and aspirations—not corporate goals. You cannot ask a toaster what it wants to become. Manufacturing predefines what will be produced. We are working with humans who have a free will and desires beyond our understanding.

> "To feel alive, to be interested and engrossed in an activity, to be in a state of flow, is all well and good," some will say, "but what does it get you?" These people want results. They want "noteworthy pictures," and they don't care whether the painter is in "a high state of functioning" while creating them. They want high test scores, and they are not terribly concerned if the students feel good or

are interested in school. They want profits, and they do not pay much attention to the professional or personal development of the employees.[21]

WHAT IS THE MEASURE OF A SUCCESSFUL PERSON?

Is making the most money our definition of a successful person? Does competition satisfy what all humans long for? Do higher test scores guarantee America's having the competitive edge? The answers are no, no, and no. Perhaps a better definition of success is a student's ability to be compassionate, listen well, network with others, bring tasks to completion in working individually or on a team, and be a positive influence on others.

Why are we wrestling with what fails to satisfy? The truth is all around us, but we are just too frightened to take the risk of really investing in people on their own terms. A healthy nation and a healthy world will only be made with healthy individuals. The Business Roundtables may have the finances but not necessarily the wisdom and the vision of what freedom and democracy in the classroom can do for all. Business has no business in education's business.

Data worship results in a myopic view of what the world could and should be. Children, we might remind corporate America, are more than math and science scores. While math and science play important roles in our lives, there are other scores we might help children increase: their creativity score, their empathy score, their resiliency score, their curiosity score, their integrity score, their thoughtfulness score, their take-initiative score, their innovation score, their critical thinking score, their passion score, their problem-solving score, their refusal to follow leaders who lie to them score, their democratic engagement score . . . and so forth. . . .

Despite their "failure," the U.S. remains the sole global superpower, houses twice as many Nobel laureates as any other country, has the most productive workforce on the planet, and leads the globe in innovation. I'd also argue that the average U.S. citizen is a decent and humane person. None of this is possible without the infrastructure, and genius, developed and supported by public education.[22]

6

Oppressing Freedom and Creativity

Education either functions as an instrument which is used to facilitate the integration of generations into the logic of the present system and bring about conformity to it, or it becomes the "practice of freedom," the means by which men and women deal critically and creatively with reality and discover how to participate in the transformation of their world.[1]

—*Paulo Freire*

Throughout our lives, most of us are taught the proper use of our free will. We are told we cannot do whatever we want, whenever we want. Freedom is not license. There are family, community, and societal norms that encourage us to live civil lives. There are penalties for those who act lawlessly. The hope is that somewhere in our development we can see the reason why we should conform to some societal standards and challenge others.

The opportunity to make these decisions comes with practice. The family unit is where it begins. Depending on levels of maturity, parents often give children the options of exercising their free will within the bounds of parental authority. In some areas a child can choose among a set of options; in another they cannot.

As they grow so does the tension between parent and child. The child struggles to gain more and more autonomy, and the parent slowly gives up control until adulthood has been reached. Whether or not this ideal scenario has been followed, most children do reach adulthood with some sense of autonomy—the proper exercise of free will in making decisions.

FREE WILL AND AUTONOMY IN SCHOOLS

Formal education needs to support this process from kindergarten through high school. Schools are intended to be an extension of the parents during school time and beyond with both assignments and after-school activities. It is that first step into public life where, within the confines of the classroom and the school, each child has the opportunity to practice choice within the given rules and regulations.

Generally, more and more freedoms should be given to students as they progress through each grade level. Teachers should recognize what they can trust each student to do without excessive monitoring. Teachers' authority is validated as they request what is reasonable and treat each student with respect. Just as in the family, the teacher should create lessons where students have the opportunity to exercise their autonomy within the classroom.

Students should have the freedom to ask questions and share their opinions. It is also healthy for students to sometimes challenge what is being taught and/or classroom procedures and policies. This is a welcome sign of engagement in the learning experience. They also should be given some choices when doing projects and presentations that are expressions of their individuality. Within the curricular guidelines of the school they should be able to choose some electives along with those courses that are required. Proper development of free will involves the opportunity to exercise it as well as the opportunity to give it up to law and authority.

> A delegation led by the Consortium for School Networking (CoSN) recently toured Scandinavia in search of answers for how students in that region of the world were able to score so high on a recent international test of math and science skills. They found that educators in Finland, Sweden, and Denmark all cited autonomy, project-based learning, and nationwide broadband Internet access as keys to their success. What the CoSN delegation didn't find in those nations were competitive grading, standardized testing, and top-down accountability—all staples of the American education system.[2]

OBLIGATION AND INDEPENDENT THINKING AT HOME

Students should have modeled at home all the varied ways in which parents live autonomous lives. Students who continually experience parents who make it known in a disproportionate manner that they "have to go to work," "have to take care of the kids," "have to" do this, that, and the other, soon get the message that life is to be lived only under obligation.

When parents are struggling to make a living, time and energy is spent on what is necessary for survival—mostly "have tos" and fewer "want tos." It is not unusual that this paradigm is passed along to the children. This may, in fact, be the way it is with many of our poor. Parental freedom and flexibility is limited by the demands of labor-intensive work and low pay.

While in some venues this may have value, it also does little to foster independent thinking and creativity in children. Following what parents believe is their responsibility and duty is surely critical to good parenting, children also need to experience the ability to choose among options.

HIGH-STAKES TESTING AND LIMITING CHOICE

Continually being subjected to a regimen of regulation and limits suppresses the human exercise of free will. This is not the way most people want to live. Education has often been touted as a way out of poverty. By being educated, students should be increasing their options for what they would like to do in their lives—a balance between "want tos" and "have tos."

This scenario sounds as if it would work well for both advantaged and disadvantaged children. Everyone should win with a good education. A cooperative effort of helping to develop each student's autonomy sounds wonderful. Parents and schools should work together in providing age-appropriate opportunities for students to make choices and decisions regarding life inside and outside school.

As ideal as this appears, it is not currently the dominant experience. While parents may well be maintaining their portions of the effort, schools are not. With the imposition of high-stakes testing for both state and national accountability systems, student choices are being seriously stunted.

What is the purpose of public education? Historically, it has been to make good people, to make good citizens, and to nurture the individual's talents and skills. However, over the past 100 years, these noble principles have been kicked aside in lieu of a sterile testing agenda set by politicians that has ignored the needs, wants, and dreams of students, families, and local communities. If schools do not reach certain numeric benchmarks set by bureaucrats, they will be closed.[3]

NONEDUCATORS DICTATE SCHOOL AGENDA

State and federal lawmakers have ratified educational accountability testing systems, such as California's Standardized Testing and Reporting Results (STAR), Florida's Comprehensive Assessment Test (FCAT), and, at the federal level, No Child Left Behind (NCLB). Each tells school districts what to teach (standards) and how that teaching will be monitored (high-stakes test scores).

"High score acquisition" is the mantra district leaders push onto its principals, teachers, and students. Many districts then set up course or classroom pacing charts and scripted lessons that tell teachers what they should be teaching each day—sometimes each hour—(pacing) and what specific words to say and activities to follow in each lesson (scripting). What is wrong with this picture? Where are the students? What role do they play? This and similar models assume that if you have a set amount of time with accompanying words and actions that all students will learn. Anyone with a lick of teaching experience knows this is not possible.

Current state, district, and school site operations are an extension of TQM and OBE (total quality management and outcome-based education—chapter 5). It is a manufacturing model applied to schools. It assumes uniformity of raw materials (identical students) processed with workers (teachers) who use repetitive programmed motions (standards, pacing, scripting) and whose intent is to produce identical items (educated students) with no variation among them.

This system takes away the autonomy of teachers to modify and adjust lessons, to be creative and innovative in response to the types of students in their classes. While schools claim they encourage "differentiated instruction"—that is, instruction tailored to different types of students—the structure of pacing and scripting mitigates against it. Teachers are told what to teach, how to teach it, and how long to teach it. The focus is on the "it" and not on the student.

> I walked into the kindergarten classroom with the school's superintendent and the principal. The well-behaved children in their plaid uniforms were discussing butterflies with their teacher. Then, as we left the room and entered the hall, the teacher rushed after us with a panicked look on her face and apologized: "I'm sorry. We had finished our lesson early, and one of the children asked if he could bring his caterpillar to school, which led us to a discussion of how caterpillars turn into butterflies."

At first, I couldn't figure out why the teacher was apologizing and why her supervisors looked so displeased. And then I understood: This young teacher was worried because she had committed what is considered taboo at this particular private school. She had gone off script. In seizing what she saw as a teachable moment, in spontaneously allowing the children to discuss the process of metamorphosis when she was scheduled to be teaching something else, the teacher knew she was in danger of receiving a negative evaluation and perhaps losing her job.

If higher test scores are achieved by mandating that teachers follow a script and eschew spontaneity and passion, we will find few great teachers left in the classroom.[4]

BE PROFESSIONAL OR BE OBEDIENT?

Most teachers do not just have state testing to prepare their students for, but district benchmark tests as well. Benchmark tests are usually developed on the local level to make sure that teachers are pacing correctly in getting ready for the state tests. It is testing to get ready for more testing.

Students see their teacher's time and energy being spent on what is necessary for survival in this educational climate—mostly "have tos" and few "want tos." They see the angst many teachers work under, as they are required to say and do things contrary to their professional judgment and the professional teaching standards promulgated in their state. As an example, here are the appropriate portions of the California Standards for the Teaching Profession:[5]

Standard for Engaging and Supporting All Students in Learning

- Teachers use a variety of instructional strategies and resources that respond to students' diverse needs.
- Teachers facilitate challenging learning experiences for all students in environments that promote autonomy, interaction, and choice.
- Concepts and skills are taught in ways that encourage students to apply them in real-life contexts that make subject matter meaningful.
- Teachers assist all students to become self-directed learners who are able to demonstrate, articulate, and evaluate what they learn.

Standard for Creating and Maintaining Effective Environments for Student Learning

- Teachers encourage all students to participate in making decisions and in working independently and collaboratively.

- Teachers make effective use of instructional time as they implement class procedures and routines.

Standard for Understanding and Organizing Subject Matter for Student Learning

- Teachers organize curriculum to facilitate students' understanding of the central themes, concepts, and skills in the subject area.
- Teachers use their knowledge of student development, subject matter, instructional resources, and teaching strategies to make subject matter accessible to all students.

Standard for Planning Instruction and Designing Learning Experiences for All Students

- Teachers establish challenging learning goals for all students based on student experience, language, development, and home and school expectations. Teachers sequence curriculum and design long-term and short-range plans that incorporate subject matter knowledge, reflect grade-level curriculum expectations, and include a repertoire of instructional strategies.
- Teachers modify and adjust instructional plans according to student engagement and achievement.

State teaching standards, such as these in California, require teachers to exercise their professional autonomy in organizing, planning, sequencing, and designing lessons dependent on the variations in their students. But the testing milieu embedded with mean accountability strips them of these fundamental directives. The current climate forces teachers to behave as automated assembly-line workers. While divergence from content standards, scripts, and pacing is punishable at the site and district levels, the state professional teaching standards are not given precedence and in many cases are ignored.

When I began teaching, I taught Shakespeare, Dickens, Poe, Hawthorne, poetry, creative writing, and business writing. I taught my students to fill out employment applications, create resumes, and understand symbolism in literature. I took joy in watching them grow throughout the school year. I have always received excellent evaluations and have been well thought of by my students, their parents, and my peers.

Now I teach FCAT prep—only. It's still called English, but it isn't. I was given an instructional calendar at the beginning of the school year that laid out, week by week, which FCAT skill I was to cover in that week. I was told not to use the literature books in which our county invested thousands of dollars only a few years ago. I was told not to teach a novel and to concentrate on FCAT-length nonfiction passages. I was also told that I was to be providing direct instruction, every day, from bell to bell.

I have been "caught" twice this year allowing my students to read FCAT passages silently and respond to FCAT questions. I was told, verbatim: "Your room is too quiet." I was told they should not be reading silently in class. (Um . . . isn't that what they are required to be able to do on the test?) I was also told that I was not saying the word FCAT enough during instructional time. Now I am being told that my reappointment for next year is in question for the above transgressions. Meanwhile, my students are sick of hearing about FCAT.

They are sick of my reading to them or to each other and actually beg for silent reading time. A student asked me last week why we can't read *Romeo and Juliet*. I don't dare sit down at my desk during the class time, even to take attendance. My administration's requirements of me have become so bizarre they do not make any sense, even from a test-prep standpoint. Regardless of my reappointment for next year, I will be leaving at the end of this school year. Enough.[6]

Put teachers in a cage and they inevitably will lock their students up, too! The more teachers believe that they have some control over their classroom environments, the freer they will be to pass on this creativity and freedom to their students.

Left behind, too, are teacher autonomy and professional discretion. Now whole hallways of fourth-grade classes are on the same page of the same scripted lesson at the same moment that any supervisor should walk by, supervisors who are identically trained to look for the same manifestations of sameness, from bulletin boards to hand signals to the distance that children are trained to maintain from one another as they march to lunch, with their arms holding together their imaginary straightjackets.[7]

DO WHAT YOU ARE TOLD

Students in turn experience schools as a place that treats them as objects rather than subjects. Their value is in the test scores they produce for the teacher, school, and district. Their freedom is limited to do whatever the district-mandated and overly constricted paced and scripted lesson plans say to do.

National Center on Education and the Economy's mission is to develop policies on education and human resources. It developed out of the Carnegie organization. Its Board of Trustees include Michael Tucker (president), Mario Cuomo, Ira Magaziner, David Rockefeller, Hillary Clinton, and Vera Katz.

In 1990 this nonprofit group published "America's Choice: High Skills or Low Wages." It described the workplace as one "managed by a small group of educated planners and supervisors [utilizing] . . . administrative procedures [that] allow managers to keep control of a large number of workers. Most employees under this model need not be educated. It is far more important that they be reliable, steady, and willing to follow directions." . . . Why? Because, the report states, "More than 70 percent of the jobs in America will not require a college education by the year 2000." . . . What is needed is "Workers who do what they are told, with a good attitude," says Ron Sunseri. How do you get them, Sunseri asks: "Start now teaching students, from the earliest grades, the attitudes and social behaviors that will please business and avoid a broad-based, high-quality, academic education."[8]

The focus is on suppressing independent thinking in an educationally confined environment. This unduly denies student choices in what should be grade- and course-appropriate and life-after-school-appropriate options. The quest for higher test scores binds administrators, teachers, and students. Each loses the autonomy and freedom to apply creative solutions to new educational situations. Students do not learn how to properly manage choices and options, because the focus is on being obedient to the dogmatic program each school has instituted to raise test scores.

Recall that psychologist Robert Sternberg called our high-stakes testing programs "one of the most effective vehicles this country has created for suppressing creativity."[9]

HIGH SCORE QUEST REDUCES OPTIONS

Significantly reduced electives in science, music, social studies, vocational programs, and the arts are common. Students who score low on math or English tests are given more time on the same test prep drills and denied choices in taking electives in which they have interest. In the meantime, those who score higher are afforded those elective options. This is another example of denying the poor, who already have limited enriching experiences, the opportunities to enhance their interest and motivation to learn.

Little time and few resources are made available for field trips and play for many of the low scorers. Restricted recess even further erodes the opportunity to teach proper interrelational skills where the exercise of free will is perhaps at its greatest. Rather than broadening, their learning opportunities are reduced.

> The state should provide us with a few additional numbers. How many students cry before, during, or after the test? How many teachers leave their school or the profession because of the tests? How many exceptional children are improperly evaluated by these silly tests? How many students will be pushed, by failing the test, into summer school, a retake of the test, or a remediation program, all of which are wasteful and useless? How much valuable instructional time, for science, social studies, the arts, and creative thinking activities, will be lost because teachers are forced to teach to the test?[10]

Those students who do not fit are marginalized and even further restricted in their choices. Students will be forced to take twice the number of math or English classes with the hope that this will improve their score during the following year's testing. This is like the production line widget that does not conform to specifications: It is either considered waste to be discarded or must be continually reprocessed. Many students drop out when they believe they cannot fit in.

CREATIVE TEACHERS WILL DECLINE
Word will continue to spread through teacher graduate schools and in the community that to be a teacher is primarily to prepare students for testing and more testing. The result of this is preservice teacher disillusionment. The best practices and creativity that they are learning at the university and are eager to apply in the classroom will not be welcomed when they are hired.

There will be an increase of teachers who leave the profession within the first five years, and veteran teachers will themselves be retiring at greater rates. Applications to teacher colleges are already on the decline. Schools will more and more attract teachers who prefer to be obedient to pedagogically weak, inflexible, unimaginative teaching that requires strict adherence to the high-stakes testing rules and directives.

This new generation of teachers will be trained by their employing districts to believe in the high-stakes mantra: "Follow the pacing chart and scripted lessons in preparing students for local and state testing. If you do the same thing to all students they all will learn in exactly the same way. One size fits all."

> The goal, Perlstein shows, is to limit teaching to ideas, skills, and knowledge that can fit inside the confines of a multiple choice test. Teachers must follow a strictly paced and worded script that even mandates what classroom posters can be hung. Students are similarly regimented: Creativity and spontaneity only get in the way of data collection. And so the author treats us to the awful moment when bright kindergartners identifying long vowel sounds are told to stop—because rigid lesson plans say they are supposed to know only short vowel sounds.[11]

Teaching then becomes simple. It is not messy with having to respond to individual student needs and modifications in lesson plans as real life events should dictate. Just follow the script at the proper pace. Teachable moments are lost. The here-and-now relevant events in the life of the students are ignored and supplanted by what will be on the district and state tests.

> The debate at Sunkist [school] highlights a larger issue about increasing pressure on educators to boost student test scores. The result, many teachers say, is a frustrating lack of freedom in how they are allowed to teach, even when their individual styles have proven successful. District officials would not comment specifically on the clash, saying it's a private personnel matter. "Generally speaking, though, it is important to us that our teachers follow the guidelines set by the district," said Suzi Brown, spokeswoman for the Anaheim City School District.[12]

WHAT ARE WE DOING?

Students only go through our K–12 system once. Students are learning what society outside home is all about through our schools. Day after day, year after year, they are experiencing our mechanized version of learning that is focused on tests, tests, and more tests. Widgets do not have the freedom to roam around on the assembly line—no free will expressions allowed. They must toe the line. If the message we give students is that we cannot trust them to make free will choices that sometimes are successful and sometimes fail, we are losing the very fabric of creative invention.

How is lockstep education responsive to their individual needs? It isn't. We are creating a nation of students waiting for the next set of directions, afraid to launch out on their own. Is this the type of citizens we are helping to mold? Is this the type of "education" we want for our children?

In fully embracing a high-stakes standardized testing regime, we are subverting a substantial part of what makes America unique and productive: our ingenuity, our self-reliance, our faith that we make a better tomorrow through creativity and collaboration, not conforming to others' ideas about what we ought to know or be able to do. Instead, we are being asked to stay passively in our chair and make a selection from answers provided, obey all commands and regulations no matter how punitive, ridiculous, or restrictive: blithely accept the accuracy, fairness, and lack of transparency surrounding the exams, and voice not a single word in opposition to the entire noxious enterprise.[13]

7

Student Anguish

It's harder to set the mind of a slave free than to release a body from its chains.[1]

— *Jean-Pierre Prevost*

The opposite of love is not hate—it is indifference. Indifference to the plight of students is not acceptable on the national, state, or local levels. We cannot be unresponsive to how the high-stakes testing regimen is abusing our children. As we saw in the previous chapter, radically reducing student autonomy is the first step to this abuse.

Our high-stakes testing educational system neglects students in two ways. Abuse is often thought of in terms of what one person does to another. But just as important can be what is denied to another. These are the educational travesties of commission and omission. Learning is an intensely personal experience. No matter how well conceived a state's learning standards, how well intended a district's teaching programs, how well monitored a school's test score results, or how creative a teacher's lesson plans—all are designed to impact a collective group of students.

These actions presume that each individual student in the group will respond to the same stimulus in the same fashion. This is far from the truth. Teachers are following both their professional and personal values when they give special attention to those who need an altered approach to learning. This is often called "differentiated instruction." It is the moral imperative to respond to individual educational needs within the context of a standard classroom. In this almost daily situation when the teachers are given the latitude to use their professional judgment to modify and adjust lessons, the student stands the greater chance of success.

PERSONALIZED LEARNING LOST

The high-stakes testing regimen significantly reduces this professional mandate and moral imperative to personalize learning. The focus on the classroom instruction is to teach the state's standards, because that will be on the local and state tests. This myopic view of learning sanitizes the classroom environment into formulas of scripted lessons, rigid conformity to standards, and pacing for completion according to an external timetable.

Here is where the manufacturing model of total quality management (TQM) and outcome-based education (OBE) make themselves most strongly felt. Neither takes into account the attributes of the students as a group in each particular classroom and the nature of the individual students therein. This scenario brings to mind an image of herding cattle along a trail to market. The state testing laws whip the districts who whip the schools who whip the administrators who whip the teachers who whip the students to prepare for the testing.

The only outcomes considered successful (OBE) are those that produce higher test scores and greater percentages of students who score as proficient or better (TQM). The school curriculum is focused on strategies that are believed to hammer home what will be covered on the tests. There is, most shockingly, no corroborating evidence that these tests really do tell the truth about what a student knows and is able to do.

The incredulous thing about the discussion of what the test "data" means is that the "data" means nothing. It is the interpretation of this test "data" that can be swung and twisted to support or deny a given position. Rational discussion is not possible when interpretation is prejudiced by a political or economic agenda.

Some want the "data" to validate what it believes will support its position. It becomes a self-fulfilling prophecy. What the scientific community has done to try to reduce this possibility is to encourage numerous scientists to not only try to reproduce conclusions and inferences about newly discovered phenomena, but also to develop many alternate means of validating its results. They publish these with peer review for authentication and invite criticism and/or confirmation.

HIGH-STAKES TEST SCORE INFERENCES NOT CORROBORATED

Contrary to this fundamental scientific principle, standardized testing score results stand alone without validation. It is presumed that they tell the truth about what students know and are able to do. They may in fact do nothing of the kind. There are no other means used to see if students really do know how to find "the slope of a line" and understand what it means. There is no evidence to require the students to explain what they did to arrive at the answer, no demonstration of application of slope, or whether or not they guessed at the answer without comprehension.

Only when we are able to convince decision-makers that these test scores say nothing without validation by other types of experimental designs (information-gathering processes) can we expose this insanity for what it is. By continuing to argue about conflicting pieces of numerical data and their interpretations, we give power to the whole system that thrives on this ultimately unscientific enterprise that claims validity.

TOWARD MORE VALID INFORMATION

What are the means that do get closer to the truth about student knowledge and skills? How does the classroom teacher fit into this qualitative and quantitative data-gathering process? How do performances and outside-the-classroom activities give credence to understanding? Which processes reduce anxiety and reveal more of what students really can do?

Why are summative assessments (tests at the end of a learning experience) deemed to be the pinnacle of truth when a student's daily revelation of their learning (formative assessments) is an ongoing testimony of development? What evidence is there that high-stakes teaching to the test learning lasts beyond the testing days? There is none.

Following a student's educational journeys on a daily basis provides much more information on which to make decisions on what they know and are able to do. This is just being fair to them. Although this is not the Olympics, in the end, it is treated as such. In using high-stakes testing, only the final performances count. Within the limits of the track lines, the gymnastic apparatus, the courts, pools, and fields, athletes are asked to perform tasks that have been predefined for their sport. Participants choose what activity they are best at and initiate their competition.

Students do not have that option. They do not have the choice of even selecting methods that best reveal their learning. It is made for them. The high-stakes test makers do not care about what students did yesterday, last week, or last month. The annual testing window is the only opportunity they have to perform.

INDIVIDUAL STUDENT LEARNING PREFERENCES IGNORED

The high-stakes test makers do not care about students' mental or physical conditions. The designers of the test do not care about students' learning styles. There is no thought as to what is the best way of getting the truth from each student. They believe that the testing format (in the vast majority of cases, multiple choice) is student-learning-style-neutral. It's not.

High-stakes test makers believe that the silence required during the test is best for all. They believe that, whether timed or not, since it is the same for all, it plays no part in the assessment of students' learning. They believe when one student in the testing area finishes and puts down his/her pencil, that this has no effect on the remaining students who see this.

Through the work of Carl Jung, as well as many others, it has been well validated that all humans have preferences of behavior, and beyond that, one's learning styles are based on these preferences (Jung, 1921; Eysenck, 1953; Briggs-Myers and McCauley, 1989; Keirsey and Bates, 1978; Benziger, 1989, 2000; Hirsh and Kumerow, 1989; Lawrence, 1979).

The Myers-Briggs Type Indicator (MBTI) is a personality style sorter. Its purpose is to enable one to begin to investigate the various aspects of one's Jungian preferences. It is only after fully understanding the key elements of this typology can a person "own" them. One does not have to take a sorter to help discover his/her style, but it is an aid in elucidating the concepts and provides a starting point.

As in Filbeck and Smith, this study indicates that students differ in their learning styles. These learning styles are related to students' MBTI personality types. Given that 67 percent of the sampled students in this study are feeling, sensing, and thinking students, it becomes necessary for instructors to incorporate more multiple-choice theory questions in their tests. Coincidentally, intuitive students perform best in multiple-choice theory tests compared to other test formats. The logical conclusion from these results is that students' performance, measured by test grades, can be influenced by the test format.[2]

INTROVERSION AND EXTRAVERSION IN LEARNING

According to Jungian personality typology, a person has either a preference for an introverted (I) or extraverted (E) attitude or disposition. While both are present in each of us, every person is more himself or herself in either one or the other. An introvert is energized from the inside, like a laptop computer getting its energy from its internal battery. They are more at home with quiet and reflection on ideas.

In contrast, an extravert is energized by activity and connection with the world around them, like plugging that laptop into the wall, an external source of energy. They hear themselves think by talking out loud. They process externally. Teachers observe this in the classroom when they ask a question. Those who raise their hands most often are most often extraverts who are hearing themselves think as they answer the question.

Most introverted students hear the same question the extraverts heard, but they answer the question internally, are satisfied with their answer, and find no need to raise their hand. They hear themselves think inside. Asking for quiet during testing favors the introverts. It is their preferred atmosphere. They are at their best. Extraverts are stifled. They are not permitted to talk out loud and hear themselves think in reflecting with themselves and others.

SENSING AND INTUITION IN LEARNING

Before an introvert or extravert can process, they need input. There are two preferred ways of getting input. One is from the senses, what one hears, tastes, smells, touches, and sees. When senates (S) read the word "apple," they envision their memory of an apple in shape and color. The other way of getting input is from intuition (N). This is a projection of the mind toward associations and connections beyond the senses. When intuitives (N) read the word "apple," they see many types and colors of apples, and go beyond that to relate it to applesauce, apple pies, apple juice, and so forth. They go behind words to other possible meanings. This is why intuitives (N) are better readers. They go behind the words to possible inferences that sensate (S) do not see.

In fact, our personality affects the way we learn. Practitioners have proposed an understanding of personality type (how we interact with the world and where we direct our energy, the kind of information we naturally notice, how we make decisions) can help explain why we learn differently (Ehrman & Oxford, 1990; Ehrman & Oxford, 1995; Ehrman, 1994; Wilz, 2000). According to Ehrman and Oxford, studies investigating psychological types are promising in that they offer "an accessible conceptual framework for language trainers and learners . . . greater self-regulation and better learning performance" (1990, p. 324). . . .

In a follow-up study in 1994 on 831 FSI students, Ehrman found that "introverts, intuitives, and thinkers were better readers. Sensing types were disadvantaged for both reading and speaking." A subsequent study by Ehrman and Oxford (1995) suggested that extraverts are good candidates for good language learners as they speak out and interact.[3]

IMPACT OF LEARNING STYLES ON HIGH-STAKES TESTING

What implications do these personality types have on test performance? High-stakes standardized testing requires reading questions and prompts, and then processing the meaning of what is read all in silence. Extraverts are at a distinct disadvantage. Not only are they not permitted to read out loud, but cannot talk through their reasoning. They are not allowed to hear themselves think.

When my wife and I go to dinner, I pick up the menu and read it quietly to myself. I am an introvert. My wife reads many of her options out loud, commenting, "Gee, should I have the turkey? The chicken looks good, too." This is standard operating fare for the both of us. Silent reflection is the introvert's best friend for testing.

Extraverts need to hear themselves think. It is using their best suit. When the testing structure forbids this, they are at a critical disadvantage. Is it just and fair to have wheelchair-bound disabled athletes compete with normal athletes? Here the distinction is obvious. For those who have eyes to see, extraverts (E) and sensates (S) are similarly biased against. Just showing up for the test is to their detriment.

But, most textbook writers are intuitives, as are writers of standardized tests. Most are probably unaware that their products reflect their own intuitive way of viewing the world, their way of approaching learning tasks. Writers of pencil and paper intelligence tests, also intuitives, most likely are unaware that their tests have a bias toward the kind of intelligence they value most, intuitive intelligence (manipulating symbols, drawing inferences, and the like).

Considering the biases, there is no surprise in the fact that IN (introverted intuitive) students as a group score highest on intelligence tests, followed by EN (extraverted intuitive), IS (introverted sensate), and ES (extraverted sensate), in that order. The record of American education in the twentieth century is a record of neglect of sensing intelligence (IS, ES), the kind of intelligence possessed by the majority of American Students.[4]

TEACHER TESTING AND LEARNING STYLES

It is not just students who experience the unjust impact of their learning style on their high-stakes test performance. Their teachers also have to deal with their credentialing high-stakes tests. How can NCLB call for "highly qualified" teachers when some of the testing they must undergo may qualify others as higher than them just because of their learning style, and disregard their practical teaching skills and knowledge?

> The data were consistent with past results indicating that most teachers are classified as sensing types, and like most sensing types, they score below the intuitive types on a standardized test. It is concluded that the study confirms the importance of examining the interaction between the academic qualifications and the personality types of students in training as well as in selecting students.[5]

Most university professors are also introverted intuitive (IN) types. Many of them expect their students to function as they do. Those students who are "hands-on" (ES) types suffer in this atmosphere. While they are best when they are given the opportunity to practically apply what they know, they are weakest at manipulating symbols and ideas in a theoretical way.

> In the seven years history of this course, it was frequently noted that the theory and experiment grades did not correlate well. In order to help analyze this discrepancy, the Myers-Briggs Type Indicator inventory was administered to the class of 1997 and 1998. The results provided an extra analytic dimension and led to the conclusion that psychological types play an important role in student "performance" in (1) a highly structured classroom environment and (2) a free-structure experimental project. Traditional graduate assessment criteria heavily biased towards the classroom environment so that students with excellent hands-on and creative skills are not evaluated adequately.[6]

JUDGING AND PERCEIVING IN LEARNING

Along with the impact of introversion, extroversion, sensing, and perceiving on learning, there are the overarching functions of judging (J) and perceiving (P). These last two reveal one's approach to conducting one's life. While Jung only alluded to these two functions, Meyers and Briggs made them more explicit.

A judging-type person wants to live an orderly, structured life. They are information organizers. They go to meetings and gatherings on time, and expect to leave on time. They often park their cars in such a way as to be better able to leave an event. They care more about the beginning and end of a meeting than its quality. They value closure on experiences.

Perceiving types are information gatherers. They can have many projects going simultaneously without the need to have them completed. They often arrive late for gatherings and leave at their leisure. They care more about the quality of the meeting than its beginning or end. They tend to not to want experiences to end.

In the classroom, judging-type students usually turn their assignments in on time, more so than perceiving-type students. The quality of perceiving-type work is generally better than judging-type work, but there is less of it. Most teachers are judging types and so structure their classroom operation to fit their type. So most classroom situations favor judging-type students, and hence they are generally more successful than perceiving types.

> The J types consistently achieve higher grades for a given amount of aptitude; that is, they over achieve. The P types get grades lower than expected for their level of aptitude; that is, they underachieve.[7]

JUDGING AND PERCEIVING IN HIGH-STAKES TESTING

In high-stakes testing, the time assigned for each test is a friend to judging types. Judging types are adept at organizing their time according to what is given—whether open ended or limited. When judging types see others finishing their tests, it raises their anxiety and motivation to finish. Perceiving types will rarely believe that they have enough time. They try to do quality work and are often lagging no matter how much time is provided.

In the ordinary classroom, teachers use multiple sources of information that involve assignments and assessments that vary in such a way that provide for more fair and just evaluations of what all students know and are able to do. The normal variation in classroom activities provides a greater probability of all learning types to demonstrate some degree of competence.

Within the confines of once-a-year high-stakes testing, the variations in Jungian types give definite advantages to some types over others. As teaching has become more and more focused on test preparation, once again a more narrow set of classroom activities favor specific styles to the detriment of others. This is terribly unjust when critical decisions about students, teachers, and schools rest on these invalid test scores.

SILENT PREJUDICE
The silent prejudice that gives high-stakes testing advantages to some learning styles over others is not just based on Jungian typology but will also find support in Howard Gardner's theory of multiple intelligences as well as visual, auditory, and kinesthetic (tactile) learning styles. The fact is that these high-stakes test developers are so myopic in their construction and interpretation of resulting scores that they do not concern themselves with the uniqueness of individual students and how to best extract their knowledge and skills.

They do not care about the nature of students. Their focus is to produce a number that can then be claimed as the truth. Meanwhile, without realizing it, kids are being horribly misjudged, educators are drawing irrelevant conclusions, and parents are being sold disinformation. This really is a gross miscarriage of justice.

Educators, parents, and decision-makers should insist on multiple sources of evidence that confirms that this test score interpretation for this student tells the truth about what they know and are able to do. In fact, on the California Standardized Testing and Reporting Results (STAR) reporting form[8] sent home to parents, there is a cautionary note that is rarely read and understood:

> HOW SHOULD I USE THESE STAR PROGRAM RESULTS: These results are one of several tools used to follow your child's educational progress. While they provide an important measure, they should be viewed with other available information about your child's achievement, such as classroom tests, assignments, and grades.

This important caveat, not only expressing the limited nature of this data but also encouraging parents to seek out multiple sources of information regarding student achievement, is most often ignored. The score summaries are just mailed home in isolation and interpreted by most parents to be a summative conclusion of how well their children are doing in math, English, and any other state-tested courses. An appropriate way of dealing with student achievement information is for parents to meet with their children's teacher(s) to review all of their academic classroom progress, including a professional interpretation of their standardized testing scores.

NO SINGLE TEST CAN DO IT ALL

A diagnostic test to determine a car's exhaust emission level will not tell you if the tires need air. A different procedure will provide the mechanic with that information. The same goes for tests in education. No single test can ascertain whether all educational goals are being met.

> A variety of assessments—or "multiple measures"—is necessary to provide educators with a well-rounded view of what students know and can do. Just as different tests provide different information, no one kind of test can tell us all we need to know about a student's learning. This "multiple-measures approach" to assessment is the keystone to valid, reliable, and fair information about student achievement.[9]

STANDARDS OF EDUCATIONAL TESTING

The travesty is that the state and NCLB do not follow their own advice. They do not treat this as severely limited information; they treat it as the sole source of information and draw conclusions and make inferences that impact each student's educational life as well as that of their teachers, school, and district.

High-stakes testing scores are often called a "snapshot." Would you buy a home or a car with just a snapshot, and a blurry, discolored one at that? Professional assessment organizations as well as state departments of education know that these tests are being used most inappropriately. They have standards that say so. Although this applies to all states, here is California's testing version:

> Standard 13.7 of the *Standards for Educational and Psychological Testing* states, "In educational settings, a decision or characterization that will have major impact on a student should not be made on the basis of a single test score. Other relevant information should be taken into account if it will enhance the

overall validity of the decision." It is inappropriate to use either CST or CAT/6 Survey scores by themselves to make decisions about student placement and/or eligibility for special programs.[10]

IGNORING STANDARDS

Would you choose to be operated on by a medical team that ignored hospital standards of cleanliness for their surgical tools? Would you fly with a pilot who disregarded with impunity FAA safety standards of landing? The *Standards for Educational and Psychological Testing*—created by the American Psychological Association, the American Educational Research Association, and the National Council on Measurement in Education—present a number of principles that are designed to promote fairness in testing and avoid unintended consequences but are consistently disregarded. They include the following:

- Any decision about a student's continued education, such as retention, tracking, or graduation, should not be based on the results of a single test, but should include other relevant and valid information.
- When test results substantially contribute to decisions made about student promotion or graduation, there should be evidence that the test addresses only the specific or generalized content and skills that students have had an opportunity to learn. For tests that will determine a student's eligibility for promotion to the next grade or for high school graduation, students should be granted, if needed, multiple opportunities to demonstrate mastery of materials through equivalent testing procedures.
- When a school district, state, or some other authority mandates a test, the ways in which the test results are intended to be used should be clearly described. It is also the responsibility of those who mandate the test to monitor its impact, particularly on racial and ethnic-minority students or students of lower socioeconomic status, and to identify and minimize potential negative consequences of such testing.

Results of a single test score, rather than multiple sources of information, not only deny some students graduation and promotion, but they are also used to modify a student's daily schedule of content courses and electives. They change students' lives. Minorities and second-language learners suffer the greatest inequities and judgments based on these one-time test scores.

Those who continue to enforce the high-stakes testing mindset are either ignorant of its severely limited value or consciously indifferent to its consequences. Decision-makers are imposing their testing agenda on the educational community. These dictators of the educational agenda are making themselves the only source of truth and using fear and threats to enforce their myopic views. The imposition of their will on powerless students is indefensible. High-stakes testing is oppressing students, teachers, and the community. There is little thought of the collateral damage caused by its use.

THE PRICE THAT STUDENTS PAY

Elementary school children are in the process of finding their worth, developing their self image. This process finds its roots in family life; hopefully, parents give them the message of how valued and loved they are just for being themselves. But at the earliest of levels of schooling, children are being given the message that their importance is in what they can provide to the teacher and school with their test scores.

With the curriculum so focused on math and English (the heart of the testing), students have art, music, social studies, science, and even physical education and play either significantly reduced or eliminated. Small children are not aware of this. Schools, classrooms, and teachers are a new experience. They have little or no expectations of what they are being denied. But we do.

Many are taught by stressed-out teachers, who themselves are under the gun to improve test scores. These children know when their teachers are pressured. They can see it in the teachers' demeanor, the way they talk about the reasons for learning, which is to prepare for the tests. While some exercise is good, overdoing it can cause significant health issues. So it is with the nature of high-stakes test drilling taken to the extreme.

This process is not the exception; it is the rule. It even intensifies with those students who scored poorly on the previous testing. What do they get? More of the same. Students are shown their test scores and then told that their goal is to "improve." Does each student have a specific path to improvement? No. "Whatever you do, just score higher."

Suffice it to say that they do not receive their test scores from the spring testing until the start of school in the fall. They are now in a different grade with a different teacher and with a set of different standards. Nonetheless, the next set of scores they will receive will not be until the following fall, when they have again hopefully progressed to the next grade.

Along with this timing debacle, can you imagine the confusion and frustration on the students' part when they are not told exactly what question(s)—and their related standards—they missed. To protect the "integrity" of the test, the state does not tell the student this information.

They may not even be tested on the same standard(s) the next time they are tested. The student does not know why they missed the question. Was it because of significant or minor ignorance, misreading, language/cultural miscues, mismarking of the answer sheet, test anxiety, or even poor guessing?

How would you like to be a student who is told to improve your high-stakes test score(s) when you do not know how to strengthen any associated academic weakness(es)? Then you are assigned to extra time (classes) focused on low scorers, which does not address your particular situation. All of this is in anticipation of the next test that may not even ask related questions that you missed on the prior test. This is a student's educational hell. It is like being arrested for a crime you may not have committed, with insufficient evidence, and no lawyer to advocate for you, but you still must stay in jail.

BUBBLE STUDENTS

Another of the atrocities of this test score mania is the plight of those not identified as "bubble" students.

> The key observation is that all students in a given range contribute the same value to the score. So for example, in California, a student with a percentile rank of 45 is equivalent to a student with a percentile rank of 59. Now, if you are the teacher, which of these students is more deserving of your attention? Well, if you work hard with the student with rank 45 maybe you can get him up to 50 or even 55. But that doesn't help! On the other hand if you can bring up the rank 59 student just two percentile points she will jump a level. The rank 59 student is a bubble student. In general the bubble students are the ones around the scoring boundaries, and the school systems are training teachers to find and focus most of their attention on the bubble students.[11]

The goal of most high-stakes testing systems is to have all students attain a score of "proficiency" as defined by the state. This arbitrarily assigned score is intended to separate the haves from the have-nots. Bubble students are at the basic level and are "on the bubble," ready to jump to this proficient level during the next year's testing. Their scores are almost at proficient, but not quite.

Schools, districts, and states are judged by the percent of students who achieve this arbitrarily assigned proficient level. Teachers are often informed by school or district directives to allocate their time and resources so that those students on the "bubble" might be able to achieve a proficient score.

Meanwhile, those who are not bubble students—the high scorers and very low scorers—receive less attention. This is not differentiated instruction, but discriminatory instruction!

In the upper grades, some students know what is happening but just follow along. Parents should be incensed that equal access to learning is being denied their children—both high and low scorers.

Many low-scoring students are being told that, instead of enrichment programs open to all, they will go to "fast track," which is intense test prep. Some middle and high school students are being told that they must take remedial test prep courses (sometimes taking two math and two English classes) if they score low on math or English testing and miss out on electives they want to take—all without parent or student approval.

Most often these students are of low socioeconomic status. Why are those who are most impoverished being subjected to more deprivation? On the surface, it is made to appear that these courses and programs are intended to help these students. Help them do what? Improve on a score that may or may not happen, and that may or may not say anything valid about what it is purported to measure? No, it denies those very students who have a dearth of learning experiences in their home life the opportunity to broaden their experience of the world through enrichment activities and interesting electives.

Those high scorers who have many of these experiences get more, and those in most need get less. A student's education cannot go backward; their lives move forward. Suppressing students' desire to know in favor of programs designed to possibly improve test scores is educational malfeasance.

IMPACT ON MINDS AND BODIES

How do students' bodies and minds respond to this intense focus on high-stakes testing? How do students process the message that this testing time will be a major component in defining them, their teacher, and school, and possibly determine what courses and grades will be open to them next year and even graduation? The welfare and reputation of students is not protected, as test scores are made public on "data walls" in some schools and classrooms by numerical identifiers. Significant harm is being done to many students' developing self-worth and desire to learn.

Even if individual students' test scores are not made public, it is very evident that students have been taught well how to judge themselves if their score does not measure up. Students are very quick to paint a negative picture of themselves and fulfill a self-fulfilling prophecy. Anxiety and stress in and around testing produces meteoric rises in headaches and stomachaches, sleep disturbance, increased absences, aggressive behavior, and depression.

The lawmakers and other decision-makers who support the testing are not in the classroom. They do not know the students. They do not see the damage. We do. Where is the state and congressional investigation into student suffering and pain as a result of their high-stakes testing laws? Do they want to know? Do they care?

If these tests are so benign, why would some teachers risk their jobs and defy their districts' orders to administer the tests (see chapter 9)? What do they see that most don't? We have students who are vomiting before, during, and after testing. We have testing companies who have protocols as to how to place tests with vomit in plastic bags, but not how to compassionately respond to the sick student.

> The constant testing is painful. I lose about 8 weeks teaching time to the constant preparing, testing, and makeups. I have had the kids that have sat with tears in their eyes when they know their English isn't ready to be tested yet. I've had the kid who is so ADHD that he can feel the pressure and gets violent. I had an intervention group last year who knew they were in "the stupid group" and acted accordingly. I had the little boy who walked up to tell me he was really nervous about the test and threw up on my shoes. I totally quit giving any "tests" in my own classes. Yet, my kids read and write more than any other on campus. They can explain the subject matter to you.[12]

Here is an anecdotal sampling of comments from teachers at one local school:

> —I have a student who has been crying every morning because of testing. He just sat there and stared at his test for about 10 or 15 minutes until I encouraged

him to work on it. Even then he kept crying throughout the day. After testing time, during our reading block, I had a student who continually complained of a stomachache and wanted to go to the nurse. Every day this week he has had a stomachache. One student was absent the last day of the test. During the second day of testing he had a stomachache all day.

—Naughty behavior during testing is on the rise. We test them three times a year for our District, then we test them for the state. We test them in writing three times a year. We also test them for reading levels several times a year. In addition to that we test them in math, science, and social studies. Each time we have testing going on in the school, the students act out in more violent ways. They are mean to each other and much more noisy.

—I have been extremely stressed out. My heart has been racing, my shoulders have been in knots, and I have been exhausted trying to keep the students in line. The pressure of the test to do better than our best has been extremely high. . . . If students are not proficient or advanced we have to tell them to work harder. Some of them are working as hard as they can. . . . We expect them to master things that are well above their developmental level. Then we test them on it and expect high test scores.

MORE ANECDOTAL MAYHEM

Everyone must be tested. A "special day" class teacher at the same school has students who are from fourth through sixth grades but function at a K–2 level and are also required to be tested. She comments as follows:

The majority of my students are lucky if they can recognize a few simple sight words on these tests and they are, in fact, a complete waste of their learning time. . . . Being a waste of their time isn't the worst "fall out" from these assessments. The tests only serve to remind my students of everything they do not know, which is considerable. I have had student behavior range from tears to rage during these testing days. Expecting special day class students to take grade level exams is, in my opinion, not only wasteful but cruel.

And the school nurse at the same site sends out an e-mail to all teachers, which in part reads:

Hello Teachers . . . are you making it through testing ok? . . . There have been 78 kids who have come to the health office since 8am Monday morning and it is only 12:30 on Wednesday . . . that is over 10% of the school population. . . . I understand stomach aches are a common thing right now because of the testing stress on the kids . . . but if they are acting fine please try to hold onto them.

A limited English proficient (LEP) teacher concludes, "One of my boys, a low LEP student, said that when he was being tested this week he feels like a monkey swinging in the trees and he suddenly smacked into one. Testing hurts."

Parents comment that their daily lives have changed for the worse prior to, during, and immediately following this testing window. Activities that have been considered normal, such as polite conversation and household duties, became situations that were overly argumentative and/or ignored. We continue to allow our fear of test score results to fuel this cycle of stress and sickness-inducing assessments.

While some of us can be advocates for our children, there are many other parents who are new to our educational system and have no idea what could be happening to their children in this testing mania. There once was a commercial that asked, "Do you know where your children are tonight?" I suggest a different question: "Do I know what effect this testing is having on my child today?"

Many experts in child development link the increased pressure on young children and the decline of play to later school failure. In February 2006, a "Call to Action on the Education of Young Children," issued by the Alliance for Childhood and signed by more than 150 leading educators, physicians, and other experts, called for a reversal of education policies that cut time for child-initiated play and emphasize formal instruction.

In local districts, reduced play is being observed at some schools in shortened recess and lunch times as well as reduction or elimination of physical education, even though it is also a required state standard. The focus on improving test scores is making many students sick in body and mind. It is a kind of torture that the public is not in contact with.

Parents, teachers, school nurses and psychologists, and child psychiatrists report that the stress of high-stakes testing is literally making children sick. Kathy Vannini, the elementary school nurse in Longmeadow, Massachusetts, says she dreads the springtime weeks when children must take the MCAS—the lengthy tests now required of Massachusetts students starting in third grade. "My office is filled with children with headaches and stomachaches every day," she reports.

"One third-grader was beside himself on the morning of the test—he could not stop sobbing. I've been a school nurse for twenty years, and the stresses on children have worsened in that time. But this testing has greatly increased their anxiety level." . . . The school's counselor, she added, reports more and more students with anxiety-related symptoms, sleep problems, drug use, avoidance behaviors, attendance problems, acting out, and the like. . . .

"I am seeing more families where schoolwork that is developmentally inappropriate for the cognitive levels of children is causing emotional havoc at home," says Dr. Marilyn Benoit of Howard University, president-elect of the American Academy of Child and Adolescent Psychiatry. "The pressure on teachers to teach to tests and outperform their colleagues is translating into stressful evenings for parents and children."[13]

CONSTRICTING STUDENT BRAINS

The high-stakes testing regime not only ignores student learning styles, but denies the brain the intellectual challenge that it thrives on. The preparation for these tests restricts student autonomy, limits academic experiences to rote, scripted, and paced lessons in English and mathematics with little consideration to the arts and sciences, and reduces physical activity and play. This does nothing less than give the student the message that school is not the place to be.

The part of our brain that does the learning, the neocortex (80 percent of the brain's weight), is a pattern seeker. It wants to connect the dots, as in one of those drawing/coloring books. The brain is satisfied when solving the puzzle in connecting the dots to see a "ducky" emerge. The brain wants to figure things out. The natural tendency is to go from what is known to what is unknown. The brain is curious. Good school programs are constantly challenging its students to think critically as they engage their minds and their values. The brain feels pleasure when satisfied with the discovery of the pattern(s) it is investigating. We call this the "aha" experience.

Each of the organs in our bodies has a function. The heart pumps blood; the kidneys and liver clean the blood. The neocortex portion of the brain is the organ for learning. Severely limiting the neocortex's natural processes drives the brain elsewhere to seek satisfaction. It can be as simple as playing with a video game or as terminal as dropping out of school. Lack of appropriate mental stimulation and a despair born of repeated failure encourages the mind to seek more intellectual stimulation in nonschool venues.

This is the simple truth of brain-compatible learning in schools: If formal education does not engage the brain in its dominant function (learning), it will either direct itself to find sources of challenge or limit its focus to other pleasure-seeking activities. The high-stakes testing regime limits intellectual investigation to only what is on the test. There is little room for imagination and creativity when focused on memorization of facts and disconnected bits of information. This has been well evidenced in the response of university professors from many institutions who complain that their students no longer want to think or challenge course concepts.

What students say they want to know is how to best prepare for the course exams and little else. There is a lack of engagement. Even on the simplest level, those states that have had testing the longest are graduating students who are in most need for remediation before entering college.

> Marilee Jones, MIT Dean of Admissions: "You don't see the kind of wild inno-vation from individuals you used to see," Jones said over lunch during a recent interview. "You see a lot of group and team projects overseen by profession-als, but you don't see the kind of rogue, interesting stuff that we used to see at MIT." MIT faculty told her many students just weren't much fun to teach. The issue of perfectionism had been brought painfully to the fore at MIT by a series of student suicides. Students "want to do everything right, they want to know exactly what's on the test," faculty told her. "They're so afraid of failing or step-ping out of line, that they're not really good students."[14]

WHO WILL PROTECT STUDENTS?

Can students be protected from state testing by their parents? About twenty states let parents waive state-mandated testing (not graduation) of their children, usually without having to give a reason. While the testing days them-selves are a traumatic event for many students, the more insidious events take place during the approximately 170 other school days that are focused on preparing for the testing.

Could this letter written about the Massachusetts Comprehensive Assess-ment System (MCAS) be written by your child? A Massachusetts student, Jacob Miller, wrote it:

> To the editor: MCAS Hinders Student Learning
> This has gone way too far. MCAS has taken over schools across the state, especially mine. I am a student at the Hastings Middle School in Fairhaven, and I just can't take this anymore. Since our school received bad scores, there have

been a whole lot of changes, and most of them for the worse. For example, in every single class we have a question that we have to answer in a paragraph just to prepare us for MCAS. This was in art class. Come on! In art class, we have to write a paragraph?

School and learning has taken a back seat to this MCAS testing. Teachers can't teach freely, and students can't learn as much as they would if there was no testing at all. Before MCAS, teachers and students didn't have to worry about these things, like preparing for a test or meeting a curriculum. You just learned for the sake of learning and bettering yourself. It's just not fair to me and all the other students to have to learn like this. We go to school to learn, not to learn what MCAS tells us to learn. I am not saying that everything about the MCAS is wrong, but it shouldn't control our learning completely. Come on! We have to answer an "essential question" in gym, too.

It's just unnecessary. Also, because of MCAS, this year things like Spanish took a back seat. We have hour-long periods, so there are fewer classes. So classes like Spanish are every other day. Those are just a couple of examples, but it's just spun out of control. I bet that the adults that read this would think I am so wrong, but believe me, if you went back to school and did everything that this generation is doing, you wouldn't like it, and you would be in the same position I am—a very angry person.

It's sickening that the mistakes of adults will alter my life, and people need to realize that a mistake in education is a mistake that will have a bad affect on everyone's life and future.[15]

Students are suffering. Those who either support or ignore this student angst are the perpetrators. Enough said.

A Culture of Fear

If our educational leaders (superintendents) are silenced, what chance do our principals, teachers, parents, and children have? Since no one is willing to tell the Emperor that he is not wearing any clothes, our children continue to suffer. Our children continue to suffer because we fail to come to their defense. Our children continue to suffer because we compromise our principles. Our children continue to suffer because we refuse to listen to them, hear their cries. Our children continue to suffer because few are bold enough to utter a word in defense of them.

Our children continue to suffer because our so-called political, religious, educational, and community leaders are so weak and paralyzed by complicity or fear. Here's my charge to educational leaders. If you are not going to pledge allegiance to children, shut up and continue to do as you are told to do. Do not pretend to be an educator. Do not pretend to be free. Your children will surely follow your lead.[1]

—Bernard Gassaway

Fear is a feeling. Everyone has experienced fear in one form or another. It is part of life. Some of us are able to cope, others not. Some of us would like the rest of us to make decisions and/or exhibit behaviors in accordance with our likes and dislikes. We hope that others can see the value of our position and make a free-will action that pleases us. If they do not, we can try to convince them to reconsider; but if they still do not, we can attempt to frighten them into doing our bidding. We figure if the threat is great enough they will comply.

Support for the high-stakes testing paradigm rests not on democracy and professional opinions, but on using fear to gain perceived results. Perception can sometimes divert us from the truth. There are theories of selling in some businesses that are based on using uncertainty and doubt to fuel fear.

The solution becomes the purchase of a product or service that gives the perception that the threat is either reduced or eliminated: "Buy this insurance to protect your family in the event of your death." "Invest in this stock to protect your assets." "Our nation is at risk. We will lose our competitive edge if we do not have better educated students and educators than those other countries." Alarm bells ring.

TRIUNE MODEL OF THE BRAIN

What goes on in our brain when this happens? The human feelings of fear, anxiety, and anguish reside in the brain. Dr. Paul McLean of the National Institutes of Health has developed a well-accepted theory of a triune model of the human brain. According to this model, the brain is divided into three major portions.

The most primitive portion is the reptilian brain. It is the smallest part and has its roots in our premammalian ancestors of 250 million years ago. Its primary function is to develop means of survival and coordinate all basic bodily functions of heartbeat, breathing, and so on. In the environment it directs the search for food, shelter, reproduction, avoidance of predators, and returning home. When a person is threatened, it directs the first response. It summons the body to either fight or run away to safety. This is sometimes called the "fight or flight" brain response.

The second major part of the brain is called the old mammalian brain (sometimes referred to as the limbic system). It is a bit larger than the reptilian portion of the brain. It has its roots in our mammalian ancestors of sixty million years ago. Its primary function is to deal with relationships and emotions and act as a "broker" between the reptilian and the new mammalian brain, otherwise known as the neocortex. The old mammalian brain is that part of the brain that assesses the relational tone of the environment. If the atmosphere is conducive to harmony, it makes the activities of the neocortex more efficient.

The neocortex composes five-sixths of the whole brain. Its roots date to one to two million years ago. Its size and complexity relative to the rest of the brain set us strongly apart from other animals. Its primary function is to learn, and make plans and carry them out. It is the center of consciousness, abstract thought, language, and imagination—it "thinks."

For it to operate at its maximum performance, two preconditions must exist: The reptilian brain must report that all the basic necessities of food, shelter, and safety have been met, and the old mammalian brain must survey the environment and conclude that the relational tone is supportive. With these prerequisites, the neocortex then has the opportunity to function as it was designed to do. If either the reptilian or the old mammalian brain gives evidence that the situation is not suitable for thinking, the neocortex "downshifts" to acquire the conditions necessary for it to perform.

If a person is hungry, thirsty, or cold, he/she will seek out food, drink, warm clothing, or temperate location. The brain directs these actions to have the neocortex operate more effectively. If a person experiences derision or exclusion from the people surrounding them, the old mammalian brain will direct them to seek to change the situation or leave it for an atmosphere more conducive to harmony so that the neocortex can function normally.

EDUCATORS' THREAT RESPONSE

This triune model of the brain applies to students, teachers, and administrators. In the classroom the brain is the organ for learning. A teacher is not talking or designing activities for the liver or the lungs. This is why one of the most critical aspects of teaching is to make the classroom and its environs student-friendly—physically and emotionally safe.

You want to be the kind of person who creates a classroom and a school where students want to be. When both the reptilian and old mammalian portions of the brain are not under threat, then learning opportunities are maximized. It is the brain and all its attributes that the teacher is communicating with. It is a brain-to-brain dynamic that operates during learning. A threatened brain is a low-functioning brain.

When administrators or teachers feel their job security is threatened because they cannot produce specific test score results, their brains downshift. The reptilian brain now is induced to take radical steps to protect job security—the source of income for food and shelter. Like a dense, dark fog that envelops education, fears of reprisals and punishment regarding lack of test score production downshift all these threatened brains to survival mode. This high-stakes testing fear seems to invade many aspects of today's educational endeavor.

STUDENTS' THREAT RESPONSE

The reptilian brain takes control. In a panic, the rationality of the neocortex is compromised. Individuals either fight for survival or leave the situation; educators and students are doing both. Even though a student's body may be physically present, he/she may have mentally "left the classroom." Most students do stay in the classroom and try to deal with the undue anxiety, but many are in the process of losing their desire to learn.

It is the pervasiveness of this pressure, day in and day out, that is at work. Most of us can deal with the threat of one or two bees in the backyard. But when the entire hive is after us, we rightly panic and seek safety. Most students can cope with a little anxiety in this or that part of the school day, but when it is everywhere and apparently unrelenting, students become traumatized.

Fear of punishment is more a stimulant of effort rather than learning. In business, motivation by fear is a "do it or else we can replace you" approach. This is basically "take it or leave it." Motivation by fear is the easiest form of motivation; however, it is based on intimidation. "Take it or leave it" may get some knee-jerk results, but the worker will not be able to utilize his or her full potential.

Motivation by fear always results in inner anger against the person using the fear tactics. Students see their instructors' brains downshifting to survival status when teachers also operate in a panic mode to follow scripted lessons according to a given pacing chart. Like a virus, this teacher anxiety contracted from infected administrators is passed along to students. While teachers' and administrators' brains are physically present in school, they may not be engaged in the educational endeavor since their neocortex has downshifted to survival. They may think, "What do I have to do to get through this day?"

When they are no longer able to maintain the welcoming and emotionally safe environment for their students and themselves, their old mammalian brain downshifts to the reptilian brain and does whatever is required to do the least damage and cause the least pain.

No longer able to maintain its proper functioning, the neocortex forgoes higher-order thinking skills, creativity, and imagination. It plays it safe with teach-to-the-test protocols that take the least amount of energy with its "drill and kill" formulations.

DEMING ON THREAT

So what is happening here is that the brain is responding to the abundant threats to its well-being. Threatened district brains threaten school site administrative brains that threaten teacher brains that threaten student brains. All are in a survival mode, doing whatever they can to avoid the sanctions associated with low test scores.

Even Dr. Edwards Deming, the father of total quality management (TQM) in business practices, recognized the paralyzing impact of anxiety on employees when they work toward quantifiable targets. Remember that a bastardized interpretation of TQM in combination with "mean accountability" and outcome-based education (OBE) has become the foundation for high-stakes testing as the driver in education.

> He [Deming] urged businesses to "eliminate management by numbers, numerical goals" because they encourage short, not long-term vision.[2]

Three of Deming's criteria (he had fourteen—see chapter 5) to improve worker productivity have obvious extensions to education.[3] Deming realized that workers are no different from other people. They respond to threats used to engender fear by being less productive. The comments I have inserted in parentheses following each of these three "Deming principles" show how they demonstrate the possibility of maximizing neocortex operation of students and educators by reducing fear and fostering a positive learning environment:

- Drive out fear. People often fear reprisal if they "make waves" at work. Managers need to create an environment where workers can express concerns with confidence. (Students and educators will become more productive if they can contribute to the learning process by actually engaging the neocortex in critical thinking rather than just performing repetitive fear-motivated tasks directed by the reptilian portion of the brain. Threatening students to perform well on high-stakes testing, as well as educators' fear of reprisals, often prevent them from speaking their mind regarding policies and procedures that are contrary to best practices. This anxiety shifts the brain into a fight-or-flight mode where preservation overrides positive contributions.)

- Eliminate slogans, exhortations, and targets for the workforce. Using slogans alone, without an investigation into the processes of the workplace, can be offensive to workers because they imply that a better job could be done. Managers need to learn real ways of motivating people in their organizations. (Various forms of urging students, educators, and schools to improve their test scores are intended to motivate, but the often subtle threatening nature of them are responded to in a defensive fashion. Once again, it causes the neocortex in those who are pressured to downshift to the reptilian brain and students and educators seek to protect themselves rather than think. We often say that they are scared stiff. They become mentally immobilized. Sometimes, when teachers are told to spur their students to do "better" on the tests, this disruption of teacher-student collegiality destabilizes the old mammalian brain. With a diminished relational tone the neocortex once again is not at its best, and effective thinking lessens.)

- Eliminate numerical quotas. Quotas impede quality more than any other working condition; they leave no room for improvement. Workers need the flexibility to give customers the level of service they need. (Quotas in education are translated into test scores and proficiencies. They are a threat to students and educators. They say, "If you do not produce this number, there will be a set of penalties assigned." Scored high-stakes testing results are used to define success and failure and as such are interpreted as an assault. The brain downshifts to the reptilian brain. Students and educators are then willing to do whatever is necessary to try to make the scores and survive or just give up.)

THE BRAIN IN ALL DOMAINS

Education is a very human endeavor. It is easy to see how these parenthetical comments can apply to educators and students alike. It is not as if education should follow Deming's business practices. No. It is Deming and education who should follow the natural operation of the human brain to maximize its performance.

The same set of principles should apply to family interactions, sports, religious practices, social services, and the like. The fact is that this is how the human brain best operates regardless of the domain in which it is functioning.

Sometimes parents use fear to protect a child from harm. A child is beginning to cross a street. A car is coming, so the parent yells at the child, "STOP."

This initiates the child's brain to downshift to the reptilian brain that stops the child from crossing the street. These hopefully are rare instances. If a family uses fear to threaten a child in teaching them all acceptable behaviors, their children will be operating with a lower-functioning brain. Their neocortex will be constricted. These children will not be able to "think for themselves," because they are waiting to be threatened before they act.

> As a teacher, I know my students respond when they are encouraged, but when told they are failing and threatened with dire consequences, they tend to shut down, rather than improve. We teachers are no different. We entered this profession to make a difference. We would be far better off if we tapped that passion in a positive direction, instead of operating as if teachers need to be threatened in order to improve.[4]

Any type of system—organizations, businesses, families, and schools—can be so conditioned. The "benefit" at first appearance goes to those who are in control and use that authority to instill fear so that their preferences are carried out. The downside of this is that those in power lose the creativity, imagination, and analytical thought of the membership, whether employees, family members, students, or teachers. The more that those in leadership oppress their constituency the more stagnant the powerless become, only doing what is necessary to survive, not progress.

SOURCE OF FEAR IN EDUCATION

How does the whole educational system become infected with fear? There must be a real or perceived threat coming from somewhere. The perception from some in the business community and its government supporters is that American financial well-being is on the demise. The implication is that if America cannot compete with other countries, we will suffer—not because of our own failing business and governmental policies and practices, but because of poorly educated students. The publication of *A Nation at Risk* in 1983 initiated the corporate and governmental cry for accountability in education. The opening paragraph states:

> Our Nation is at risk. Our once unchallenged preeminence in commerce, industry, science, and technological innovation is being overtaken by competitors throughout the world. This report is concerned with only one of the many causes and dimensions of the problem, but it is the one that under girds American prosperity, security, and civility.[5]

Even though the report states that our preeminence is being challenged by many causes of this problem, the thrust of the report is that education is the culprit. It posits that if America just had a better educational system, it would be more competitive and its businesses would make more money. This is more misinformation. High international test scores do not determine a countries' economic prowess.

> Nations with strong economies (e.g., the top 22 nations on the Global Competitive Index, GCI) demonstrate a weak, nonsignificant relationship between ranks on international tests of mathematics and science achievement and economic strength as measured by GCI ranks. This conclusion is congruent with the economics literature base findings that countries with already high levels of education attainment see no effect on gross domestic product (GDP) by incremental increases in the populations' levels of education.
>
> It may be that those charged with creating and managing education policies have the capability to see and interpret the data but choose not to do so. Therefore, they give opinions (i.e., high ranks on international tests of mathematics and science bring about future economic strength) about which they know nothing.[6]

FEAR OF LESS PROFIT

Competitors are perceived by business leaders as those who are making more money than they are. They want what their rivals have. This is the meaning of competition. They want their competitors' profits. With excessive money comes wealth, power, and control. If it could be demonstrated that if all current students wore green uniforms then business profits would increase by 50 percent in five years, what do you think businesses would want for our schools? Would it make a difference to these profiteers if students who wore green uniforms also became depressed?

Business Roundtable is an association of chief executive officers of leading U.S. companies whose goal is to support the economic well-being of its membership. It is grouped in national, state, and local boards. The business roundtables and their friends are frightened. They do not want to lose what they have or any hope for a more profitable future.

They benefit by using public education as a straw man to cover business mistakes or criticism by focusing attention elsewhere. Business roundtables are grasping at education because they believe it is an economic panacea, a lifeline. It isn't. They are wasting their time and energy. They want parents to align their dreams for their children with the corporate vision of the purpose of children's education.

The corporate mantra is to push and test children according to what business believes is best for them, so that employed students might help improve businesses' competitive edge. The corporate mind does not care about individual student choice as to what each individual wants to do with his or her life. The corporate goal is to create a pool of obedient, skilled workers willing to work for as little as possible and make their employers as profitable as possible. If they can scare parents into thinking that their children are getting a poor education, then not only can they wield financial power in government to control what goes on in education, but they can also make a profit.

Public schools are civic entities (unlike businesses) and are under the control of state and national laws. Access to elected officials is easier for business interests who have the finances, lobbyists, and time to espouse their position. They are already organized in groups like the business roundtables of our country.

Individual students, parents, teachers, and schools are focused on the local issues. They are a loose array of community members focused on individual students and schools. Business can claim that schools are the problem, wrest them from the public domain, and make some profits right here at home, all the while claiming we are trying to be more competitive in the "global marketplace."

Are the fiscal crises of 2009, the near-collapse of Fannie Mae and Freddie Mac (insurers of home mortgages), the downturn in the housing and the stock market, the rise of oil prices, and the bankruptcy filings of Lehman Brothers, many banks, and homeowners due to poor student test scores? Dr. Gerald Bracey puts it very succinctly when he says in referring to recent international tests in reading, mathematics, and science:

> There is not a shred of evidence, not one shred that scores on these tests are linked to global competitiveness or other good things (Norway, considered on many variables the best place in the world to live, scores about the same as we do). The powerhouse World Economic Forum just issued its annual Global Competitiveness Report and guess who's number 1 among 131 nations: The U.S. of A. It's been that way for four consecutive years (9/11 dropped us to #2 for a bit). . . . Think about it for a minute. In four months we will "celebrate" the 25th anniversary of A Nation at Risk. In 1983, that booklet claimed we were threatened by a rising tide of mediocrity. Well, the mediocrities that graduated high school that year are now 43 and pretty much running the country. . . .

Certainly we would not have seen that fabulous economic expansion from 1992 to 2005.[7]

IS THE SKY FALLING?

False premises cannot lead to valid conclusions. In the children's fable "The Sky is Falling," Chicken Little (or Licken) is hit on the head by an acorn while eating lunch. She then runs about saying that "the sky is falling" and goes on to tell the other farm animals on her way to tell the king. The moral of the story is not to believe everything that you hear. While some business, community, and legislative members may actually believe that the academic sky is falling, others are using this perceived sense of panic to their advantage. They manipulate the disinformation of impending doom to control students, teachers, and schools.

This is done through enacting laws not based on sound educational practice, but through fear-induced tactics. State and national laws, such as NCLB, threaten states to perform or sanctions will be employed. Of course, a state, a district, and a school are each distinct mental constructs—they are not human. A state, district, or a school can't feel fear; only the humans therein can experience the attempt at frightening them into compliance.

This mindset is nicely portrayed in the article "The Case for Being Mean" (first cited in chapter 4) by Fredrick M. Hess of the American Enterprise Institute, a pro-business, right-wing think tank. The article includes this aggressive position:

> Advocates of nice accountability presume that . . . in any line of work, most employees will resist changes that require them to take on more responsibility, disrupt their routines, or threaten their jobs or wages. To overcome such resistance, we need to make inaction more painful than the proposed action. In education, this means making a lack of improvement so unpleasant for local officials and educators that they are willing to reconsider work rules, require teachers to change routines, assign teachers to classes and schools in more effective ways, increase required homework, fire ineffective teachers, and otherwise take those painful steps that are regarded as "unrealistic" most of the time.[8]

FEAR-INDUCED OPPRESSION

So the strategy is clear—frighten education into compliance: "If we can't get education to be what we want it to be, we will use suitable painful policies and practices to arrive at our goal." And who is the "we" heading up this attack on education? Business leaders and those far right-wing organizations who align themselves with fear-induced oppression.

> Shortly following the 1991 Gulf War, corporate America put another piece of territory in its sights. This time the objective was on the home front. . . . No more "frills" for young people. Art, music, and literature don't generate surplus value for defense contractors and information technology giants. The new "standards" are math, science, and technical reading. And no more real teaching. Teachers' aim now is to drill kids for the new educational bottom line—"high-stakes tests" to divide the workforce into two tiers, a high-skilled elite vs. the foot soldiers for battlefields and service industries.[9]

And if you think this is just a recent local phenomenon, back in May of 1997 a paper was produced by the secretariat for the Second Human Resources Ministerial Meeting of APEC, held in September 1997 in Seoul. The source of the paper, its content, and the process of which it is a part exemplify the reshaping of education rampant everywhere in support of the globalization of capital.

APEC stands for Asia-Pacific Economic Cooperation, a grouping of eighteen "economies" with borders on the Pacific, both in Asia and the Americas (the United States is a major player). If "APEC means business," then, as set out in this APEC paper, "Education means preparing students and educators for business." This core concept is explicit:

> The emphasis on education for itself or on education for good members of a community without a large emphasis on preparations for the future work are no longer appropriate. In other words, the idea that work is only an instrumental part of one's life is no longer appropriate. Such a dichotomist view on education and work cannot be justified in the world where economic development is emphasized.[10]

Exposed is the coercive agenda of those who believe that the purpose of education is only to serve the needs of business. Peter Henry brings this clearly into the light:

> The core of this debate over whose interests education is meant to serve characterizes a simple but important distinction in our approach to how learning actually works: On one side are people who believe that education is centered in the learner, with their interests, passions, and enthusiasm as the driving force.

On the other are people who see learning as being more about the system and adults: developing effective structures that allow the system to manage, control, and direct children to "achieve" what the system determines is important, measuring that and handing out rewards to those who comply. . . .

One side looks fearfully at young people as inputs to an economic scheme that might not be capable of achieving a minimally viable result (a la *A Nation at Risk*); the other looks optimistically at learning and seeks to maximize what students can become, create, and provide the world. Both sides say they want the best for children. Yet only one side actually takes time to ask what children want for themselves.[11]

MOTIVES EXPOSED

The big picture is now abundantly clear. There are powerful forces afoot that want to take the freedom of choice away from students. Schools are not to be sources for developing lifelong learning in whatever areas of interest students want to venture. No.

Schools are to narrow their curriculum and pedagogy to fit the needs and desires of the corporate world to produce compliant students and educators, who are conditioned by threats and fear to do what is asked of them within a very limited set of skills. Creativity, imagination, and analytical skills are reserved for those few who can afford a private education, which has the freedom to encourage those elements. As long as public schools are under the control of business interests who embrace fear as an educational motivator, our children will suffer.

> The oppressors use their "humanitarianism" to preserve a profitable situation. Thus they react almost instinctively against any experiment in education which stimulates the critical faculties and is not content with a partial view of reality that always seeks out the ties which link one point to another and one problem to another. Indeed, the interests of the oppressors lie in "changing the consciousness of the oppressed, not the situation which oppresses them," for the more the oppressed can be led to adapt to that situation, the more easily they can be dominated.[12]

We are forcing our students to live on a daily diet of academic survival. Under the dictates of those who espouse the high-stakes testing regimen, students are experiencing twelve years of fear-induced indoctrination—their brains downshifting from the fundamental learning function of the neocortex to the fight-or-flight mode of the reptilian brain: "Don't think; just do what you are told." Correctly bubbled answers are of more value than creativity and analytical thought.

If students are also surrounded by educators who themselves work under threats, is it any wonder who will be winning this battle for the classroom? Fear may be winning now, but the ultimate victory will come through those who value student interests, desires, and dreams above corporate educational manipulations. This is a goal that will not only confuse their corporate oppressors but also expose their self-serving quest for unchecked wealth, power, and control.

Student, Teacher, and Parent Redress

How Sad I Feel (or I Hate NCLB)
Oh my God, what's become of me?
My passion, my instincts, I am no longer free!
What has changed, what is wrong?
The cherishing of children, loving their "song"
Remembering the days of "TEACHING TO THE CHILD,"
The absence of this now, is driving me wild
These are children, they are what is best,
They are individuals, not robots, not a graded test!
In life we love, oh so many things
Our valuing of children, the trust and love it brings
I'm trying and I'm striving to keep teaching what is right
Treasuring children, nurturing their minds, oh so bright![1]

— *Beth Boyer*

Teachers' love for their students is seldom if ever discussed in educational literature. Love may seem too personal, soft, and mushy to be involved in professional relationships between students and teachers. But there is a lot more to it than meets the eye. Teachers are in many ways an extension of the parental role within the context of a school. There is nothing more satisfying for a parent than to know that when they send their child to school that they will be cared for by all the adults they encounter during the day—especially by their teacher(s).

What exactly does this mean? Besides the physical and emotional bond between parent and child there is the desire to be concerned for the child's well-being. This not only means protection from harm, but encouragement to learn about the world and to develop their talents, hopes, and dreams. The California Education Code declares:

> 51100. (c) All participants in the **education** process benefit when schools genuinely welcome, encourage, and guide families into establishing equal partnerships with schools to support pupil learning.

EQUAL PARTNERS

While it is assumed in this statement that families are to join schools in the child's educational process, it must be noted that it calls for "equal partnerships." This not only means that parents are to participate with schools in its role but schools are to participate with parents in the parental role. Parents mediate the world to their children. Mediation includes making meaning of things and events in the world according to each particular family's values and norms.

During a walk in the park a parent may point out a squirrel and then go beyond that to explain how important squirrels are to the environment and how valuable their place is in the park's health. The same could be said of the birds, plants, and so forth. Engendering a love of nature may be one family's value. As the child grows, this theme may be continually present in the family's activities and discussions. The same may be true of other family values, eating healthfully, and watching movies and playing games that have specific messages.

The parent monitors the child's behavior in accord with their family values. In this way, as the child grows it is hoped that those values become a part of the child. A classroom is full of twenty to forty such children. Each child comes with a different set of values; each child is hopefully loved and cared for by their parent(s) in a unique way.

TEACHERS' CARE FOR STUDENTS

Through the administration and particularly the teachers, schools are called on to show care and respect for each child, no matter what values they have when they walk into the classroom. School and classroom norms of behavior are established for the general welfare of all students. Teachers are called on to mediate these values for the good of all but respond to each student as an individual. There is an old saying for teachers: "Kids will care to know when they know that you care." This says that to some extent the desire to learn is based on a foundation of relationship expressed in the care for each student.

Recall that the organ for learning is that portion of the human brain called the neocortex. It has the possibility to operate at its peak efficiency when two conditions are met:

1. the reptilian portion of the brain concludes that the person is free from threat and has satisfied other basic needs such as food and shelter; and
2. the new mammalian portion of the brain must sense that the relational tone of the environment is positive, caring, and supportive.

Just as some students interpret parental love by particular gestures, comments, and the like, they also have a new learning opportunity in experiencing how teachers demonstrate their care and concern. Human interactions are at the core of fruitful student learning in school.

STUDENT UNIQUENESS

Students interact with their teachers approximately six hours per weekday throughout the 180-day school year. They may have quality interaction with their parents approximately three hours per day for 365 days each year. The total time of interaction with parents and teachers is comparable.

So, during the student's schooling years, teachers collectively have a similar amount of contact time with students as do their parents. What teachers make of that time with each student is as critical as what parents make of their time with their children. Another common denominator that parents and teachers share is the focus on each child as an individual. While it may be easier to treat everyone "the same," children are different and may require modified responses tailored to who they are and what they come to the classroom with.

Parents with more than one child soon become aware of each of their differing needs, desires, hopes, and dreams. This uniqueness is central to how a parent relates to each of them. This uniqueness paradigm also is critical to teachers. "Unique" not only is the nature of the interaction between each teacher and student, but it is also fundamental to establishing their relationship. Students with more than one teacher soon recognize that, like other adults in their circle of family and friends, each has a best mode of communication. So too is each teacher unique.

TEACHER UNIQUENESS

In the introduction to the California Standards for the Teaching Profession,[2] it is written, "Teaching is not a profession in which a single approach to professional practice will be effective for all practitioners."

Two of the applicable standards state:

STANDARD FOR ENGAGING AND SUPPORTING ALL STUDENTS IN LEARNING:

Teachers use a variety of instructional strategies and resources that respond to students' diverse needs. Teachers facilitate challenging learning experiences for all students in environments that promote autonomy, interaction and choice.

STANDARD FOR PLANNING INSTRUCTION AND DESIGNING LEARNING EXPERIENCES FOR ALL STUDENTS:

Teachers establish challenging learning goals for all students based on student experience, language, development, and home and school expectations. Teachers sequence curriculum and design long-term and short-range plans that incorporate subject matter knowledge, reflect grade-level curriculum expectations, and include a repertoire of instructional strategies. Teachers use instructional activities that promote learning goals and connect with student experiences and interests. Teachers modify and adjust instructional plans according to student engagement and achievement

Boiled down to its basics, this says that the teachers are unique professionals and will approach their students as unique individuals in a way consistent with these teaching standards. The ability to design, modify, and adjust lessons and then sequence them appropriately for each and every student is a most important aspect of teaching. Care of students, then, finds its practical application in response to each student's individuality. Teachers get to know their students during the course of the academic year. They discover their academic strengths and weaknesses. In time, teachers become aware of their students' lives outside school, other talents and skills, as well as their students' hopes and dreams.

STUDENTS—THE WHOLE PERSON

Teachers' care and concern for their students take them beyond each student's output in terms of classroom activities, assignments, tests, projects, and the like. What is the significant input that each student brings into the classroom? Teachers realize that they are dealing with a whole person, not just an academic person. Other issues outside and inside the school environment impact a student's ability to learn. Family life, friends, culture, and mental and physical health can have significant impact on learning.

All the feelings a student experiences contribute to who they are on any one particular day. What is a teacher to do when observing a look of sadness on a student's face as he/she walks in the room? If the student acknowledges that she is feeling sad, she is saying, "This is who I am right now." The phrase "I feel sad" is equivalent to "I am sad."

It is not a thought. One does not say, "I think sad." The student is being vulnerable and honest to whom they are. Do we say, "Sorry, you still have to take the test today?" What would parents say if their child came home looking sad and down? What would a friend say? Teachers are humans dealing with other humans. The possibility of compassion and understanding as well as indifference and rejection is always there. How we respond does make a difference. It makes a difference right then, and it makes a difference in the future.

A STUDENT'S REFLECTION ON TEACHERS

As a contributor to UCLA's Institute for Democracy, Education, and Access, Esperanza Renteria, a student at Santa Monica High in California, says this about teachers:

> Teachers are the second most influential people in students' lives. Many teachers do not know the impact that they have on their students. Quality teachers would be difficult to define because there are so many characteristics that it would be impossible to possess all of them at once. There are many quality teachers, but all with different characteristics. There are different ways in which teachers can communicate and connect with their students that make them quality teachers; however, teachers that do not connect or communicate with their students would not be considered quality teachers by their students.
>
> Teachers should care about their students, they should want to motivate and mentor their students. It is important that students see that the teacher not only cares but also believes in the students' potential. It is important for teacher to have faith in their students' potential to succeed and do well. Given that, students will feel expected to try their best, and believed in, and when somebody has hope in you, it is difficult to let them down. This is why it is important for

teachers to have faith and believe in their students, and for that they must care about them, and take their job seriously.

This could impact and motivate a student to strive for their dream, to believe in themselves, or this could push a student to lose hope, and categorize themselves as stupid or incapable. A quality teacher should know how to challenge students without making it impossible to show their virtues. This type of teacher would have to thoroughly understand each student's learning styles so he or she would be able to teach in a way in which they will not only learn but will also be intrigued by the information provided to them.

This way, teachers will be able to understand students and have the capability to reach them, and know them on a personal level, to help and mentor them. It is important that students see their teachers involved and caring, because as it is said above: Teachers are the second most influential people in their lives. With the parents being the first most influential people. They have the most ability and chance to make a difference in a young person's life. It is important that they understand this and use this to the child's benefit.

It is difficult for a teacher to be able to reach all of his/her students [on] a personal level; however, it is important they try because they need to have the students' attention and respect in order to teach them, and achieve being academically rigorous. Teachers need to be stimulating, yet intimidating at times in order to command respect. Teachers need to be patient yet motivating to grab the students' attention. It is important that teachers are able to teach without talking at the students but with them.

Lastly, a quality teacher should possess a sense of humor, an ability to laugh with his or her students and not become overly intimidating. Over all, I believe there are many types of quality teachers, but these are only some of the characteristics that I believe make up some of them.[3]

STUDENTS AS DATA PRODUCERS

Many students may not be able to articulate their need for caring teachers as well as Esperanza, but all students want to be cared about. It is comforting to know that your teachers have your welfare as a top priority. Actions speak louder than words. Students want to experience how important they are to their parents, teachers, coaches, and other significant adults in their lives.

Students want to know they have value not because of what they do and how they perform but because of who they are. High-stakes testing promotes the belief that students' importance is found in how well they score. Many students buy into this structure by judging their academic and sometimes personal self-worth on this misguided principle. High-stakes testing is embedded in a system intended to promote its own agenda: Its purpose is to gather data. This data is in the form of scores from one or more sets of standardized tests. The system does not care about the condition of the participating students. All it cares about is the data. Students are viewed as data producers.

> Under this philosophy, the student is seen by the state as a number: a TAKS (Texas Assessment of Knowledge and Skills) score, an IQ level, a passing percentage, a socioeconomic indicator, or a dropout rate. Teachers are seen as a "big brother," ensuring cheating on a high-stakes test doesn't ever occur. The numbers each child represents become the data that drives the decisions of the education process. Success is based exclusively on numbers.[4]

SCRIPTING, PACING, AND INDIVIDUALITY

This system's mindset is back-mapped into the curriculum. Suggested strategies are based on completion of a specific quantity of content within a specific time period (pacing) and saying the exact words as presented in the approved materials in a precise fashion (scripting). Both processes minimize students' individual needs and place a priority in following scripted lessons—line by line, rigidly paced hour by hour and day by day so as to finish in time for the next set of site, district, or state testing.

> "Excesses of the standards movement have promoted lock-step education," School Superintendent Michael V. McGill of Scarsdale, New York, told the *New York Times*. "They've diverted attention from important local goals, highlighted simplistic and sometimes inappropriate tests, needlessly promoted similarity in curriculum and teaching. To the extent they've caused education to regress to a state average, they've undermined excellence."[5]

The belief is that if one teaches this lesson in this specific way, in this specific time period, all students will attain the required understanding, which will then be tested. It assumes all students are the same and they all respond to outside stimuli in exactly the same way.

PRETENDING SCIENTIFIC SAMENESS

This pretends to be a scientific approach to learning. It assumes that all students in a classroom are like identical beakers of water. If you place all beakers above the same heat source for the same amount of time and measure each temperature with identical thermometers, they all will reach the same temperature at the same time. And, the thinking goes, if this does not happen, it is not because of the heating process or the effect of the thermometer in each beaker. It believes one strategy should fit all. And when this does not happen, the fault is squarely on the student and/or the teacher.

It proclaims the teaching (heating) process using scripting and pacing to be infallible and the high-stakes testing process (thermometer reading) to be valid. The high-stakes testing system believes that if you teach in exactly the same way and for the same amount of time, when tested you should get the same results from each student. It falsely pretends that there are no variations between different student needs or different teacher styles. It does not acknowledge that each student is impacted in a different way. That is of no concern. The system is sociopathic: It is callous, lacks empathy and remorse, and has no capacity to care.

It does not see itself as responsible for misguiding teachers and students. Its goal is to produce the highest test scores possible regardless of the dearth of genuine learning and the carnage it leaves behind.

> Most parents conclude that it's difficult to imagine why really great teachers, with many public and private schools eager to offer them a job, would stay at a school in which rigid lesson plans devised by others dictated how they spent almost every minute of the school day, schools in which encouraging discussions and activities generated by the children's interests and curiosity were considered pedagogical sins. . . . But if higher test scores are achieved by mandating that teachers follow a script and eschew spontaneity and passion, we will find few great teachers left in the classroom. In fact, we might as well save money on salaries and benefits and employ robots to run the drills.[6]

INDIVIDUAL DIFFERENCES

As a stark contrast to this, assume that each beaker of water holds a different volume of water and contains a unique set of dissolved minerals. Each is heated in a fashion consistent with its contents, and each temperature is measured with a different device best suited for that beaker. In this way, just like a master vintner, each barrel can become a quality wine though different and unique from any other. Yes, there is science in making wine, but the vintner is more of an artist in taking the science and applying it to each variety and vintage as the local conditions dictate.

So, when caring for their students, a teacher fits the content in a way that is adapted to them. Teachers, too, are artists. They apply their expertise, training, and classroom experience to each lesson. Their clientele leads the way. Content is presented and paced in a way that takes into account students' individual differences. Learning is assessed using a variety of methods that allow for various expressions of understanding and creativity. Evidence comes from discussions with students, projects, presentations, classroom and homework assignments, mastery conferences, and different types of assessment formats.

ONE SIZE FITS NONE

In California, as is now happening in all other states, numerous school districts will not have met the proficiency score percentages under NCLB. California state school board members visited various districts to get input before any action was taken. Juliet Williams of the Associated Press reports the following:

> A total of 98 school districts face sanctions for the first time this year for failing to meet their achievement benchmarks under the law for four consecutive years. . . . Two of the board's 11 members held a meeting in San Jose on Tuesday to get input from area districts. Members Kenneth Noonan and Ted Mitchell also will hear from districts on Wednesday in Bakersfield and Thursday in Los Angeles. "These 98 districts are where they are for 98 different reasons, and it would be inappropriate for the state to have a one-size-fits-all approach. Today reinforced that," Mitchell said following Tuesday's hearing.[7]

How can it be that the same system that supports classroom practices based on a one-size-fits-all approach with teaching and learning also rails against this mindset regarding district sanctions? Yes, it would be inappropriate for the state to have a one-size-fits-all approach to each of the ninety-eight districts. So why can't the system see that there are 49.5 million reasons why each and every student in our country deserves to be treated as a unique human being in their schooling? Because the system is not human—but teachers are.

TEACHERS SEE PAIN

So what does this one-size-fits-all approach have to do with caring for students? It places the teacher in an untenable situation. How does one reconcile the looks of confusion, frustration, and pain on their students' faces with the site and district mandate to teach in this specific way? When you love someone, it is very difficult to see him or her in pain. It is much more difficult to realize that you are the cooperating agent that inflicts the pain.

> Kathryn Sihota faces a disciplinary hearing by the Sooke School Board for refusing to give her Grade 3 class a test. Teachers were planning a rally today on Vancouver Island to support a colleague and union activist who faces possible discipline for her refusal last spring to give her Grade 3 students a district-wide reading test. Kathryn Sihota, a long-time teacher, said she has questioned the value of standardized tests for many years, but it was the tears of a student who had to write the test that convinced her to take a stand. "I'd never made a student cry before—ever," said Sihota, who teaches Grades 2 and 3 at Millstream elementary in Sooke district. "It killed me to do that [especially for] something I don't believe in." The school district says her actions amount to insubordination because the test was not optional.[8]

The high-stakes testing system lacks the compassion and understanding that teachers, as extensions of their students' parents, have for them:

> On the 3rd and final day of NCLB testing, one child starting crying during the test, and so I gently invited her to move to the rear of the classroom where she could sit by herself and have more space with fewer possible distractions. She progressively became more distraught, and refused to read or complete any further test items even though she was less than halfway finished. Minutes later, the young student lay on the floor in a fetal position, sucking her thumb, crying while asking for her mom to come get her because "it (the test) was too hard." What in the name of NCLB's inane standards are we doing to our children!! Where will this end!!! . . . I sit here tonight weeping and paralyzed by grief. I never thought I would see this day. I really didn't.[9]

TEACHERS' STRUGGLE

The system doesn't care and it wants teachers not to care—just do what they are told. No avenue is given to those who disagree. Fear of recrimination runs rampant (see chapter 8). Some teachers cooperate and do it willingly, believing in the system's misnamed "scientific" approach. Some do it grudgingly; all the while their insides are in turmoil as their student-centered values conflict with what they are told to do. Some become activists in battling systemic powers that enslave teachers and students to this process. Others cannot stand the pain and internal conflict and so leave teaching rather than continuing to do harm to their students and themselves:

> I retired last June after 39 years of teaching. I could have gone on, but I had to get out, as I totally disagree with the direction that education has gone. . . . The pressure never lets up, and the scores are never high enough. Teachers are frantic and pass this pressure on to the children. There's not enough time in class to prepare for every test, so lots of homework is given, and teachers depend on parents to help. It is not right, and many teachers are sick about having to do this. For me, this year is heavenly, to be out from under the stress of that job (which I used to love). Parents need to back the teachers in their fight against No Child Left Behind, which is not working and has taken every ounce of fun out of education.[10]

PARENTS DON'T KNOW

Where are the parents? Do they really know the short- and long-term effects of what their children are experiencing? Do they have access to a process that could effect the change their children deserve? Their instinct to protect is thwarted, because in most cases they do not even know that their children are in harm's way.

As a parent of five children and having observed other parents, I believe that parents are built to be more sensitive to short-term threats, protecting children from being bullied or picked on by other kids; placing medications and harmful chemicals in hard-to-reach locations; taking care of obvious colds, flu, cuts, scratches, and broken bones; and responding to hurt feelings, rejections, and disappointments. We are less sensitive to the long-term effects of whom our children are associating with, the quality and quantity of the TV programs they watch, books and magazines they read, the air they breathe, water they drink, the types of food they eat, and, of course, diseases that we do not have the skills to detect.

Once parents become aware of the harmful effects of fats and sugars, second-hand smoke, and those other factors that they have control over, they may begin some kind of remediation. Often, through the media and contacts with professionals, health issues such as air and water quality and long-term illnesses or diseases come to parents' attention. And when they do, parents usually have to rely on outside organizations and professionals to help remedy the situation. The level of their response is in direct proportion to the degree of severity explained to them by those in the know, whether doctors, government agencies, or other trustworthy sources.

The parent(s) must believe what these professionals are saying. Without respect and belief in their expressed concerns, parents would not be motivated to protect their children. When a parent takes his/her child to a doctor for a health checkup, they expect a professional response to whatever conditions are discovered. They would anticipate a description of the malady as well as a set of options for healing. Each option would have its strengths and weaknesses, side effects, and the like. After consultation and with the parent's permission, treatment begins. It is monitored and results are discussed with parents.

During this era of high-stakes testing, in dealing with the educational health of one's child there is no consultation on the possible effects of both the year-long preparation for the testing and the testing itself. When parents bring their children to school, they have the right to expect professional care from their teachers. They assume that their children will be treated as individuals and will be educated with the most current teaching practices. Some are willing to challenge the system when their children's education is at risk.

> Parents upset with the transfer of a fourth-grade teacher involved in a dispute with administrators over her teaching style took their students out of class and picketed in front of Sunkist Elementary School on Wednesday. They are upset that teacher Amy Asaoka-Nakakihara was transferred out of her fourth-grade class in the middle of the school year. They are demanding that the school district allow her to return to class.
>
> "She is such a passionate teacher and we see the improvements in our children. We just want her back," said parent Gina Nuñez, who marched in front of Sunkist with her son, Joseph. . . . The debate at Sunkist highlights a larger issue about increasing pressure on educators to boost student test scores. The result, many teachers say, is a frustrating lack of freedom in how they are allowed to teach, even when their individual styles have proven successful.[11]

TEACHERS RISK TELLING THE TRUTH

The high-stakes testing regimen has other ideas. It has a plan for their children before they are even seated in the classroom. That plan is to be carried forth by the teacher as an employee of the district. It directs the teacher, "This is what you will do, and how you will do it and in this time frame." If teachers are conflicted because of what they know to be best for each child, they most often will not inform the parents. They are afraid of repercussions from the site administration and district if they tell the truth to the parents.

> David Wasserman, the Sennett Middle School teacher who was threatened with firing when he refused to administer one of those questionable No Child Left Behind tests, needs to be commended for having the courage to open a few eyes. Wasserman eventually administered the Wisconsin Knowledge and Concepts Exam when he learned his protest was a firable offense. He was prepared to accept a reprimand, but, like most of us, he needs his job and the family health insurance that goes with it. . . . Maybe—just maybe—teachers like David Wasserman can wake them up.[12]

PROFESSIONAL ASSESSMENT NIXED

There is no freedom for a teacher to say to a parent, "The type of rote, superficial, noncritical test prep activities that fill your child's day are contrary to my professional opinion and are doing your child educational harm. Not only is there harm in what I am doing, there is also harm in what I am not doing. I am not focusing on science, social studies, the arts, and physical education with equal time and vigor as is spent on math and English. They read only out of a basal reader rather than age-appropriate literature. I am being directed to spend more energy on English and mathematics because that is what our test scores are based on. There is no time for them or me to be creative in their learning. I am teaching your child that going to school is all about preparing for the next standardized test. I am watching your child's desire to learn die on the vine."

This type of professional assessment is rarely told to parents, because it is not the "company line," and teachers are afraid of reprisals if they do. Tell the truth and there will be a price to pay. Most teachers do not want to risk their jobs by being written up for insubordination or being transferred and/or demoted. Some parents know this.

> This is not a case or a time in which to "balance" opinions. I say this because I know you are aware of how frightened and oppressed the teachers are by the manner in which the schools, counties, districts, and states enforce the policies of NCLB. The teachers are being gagged. I know you know that they really

CAN'T speak out about the tragedy that is their professional life or the impact of this on their students, our children. In this case, it is impossible, even if some teachers are willing to talk to you, for you to get any word from the thousands upon thousands of teachers who are too afraid to speak, or be quoted, or write. And remember, there are thousands who we don't even know how to reach. So, there is no balance to be had.[13]

The terrible downside of this is that most parents never know of the slowly evolving damage that is being done to their children, and if they ever find out it may be too late. Students only go though our school system once. You can't say, "Oops, sorry, let's go back and start over at kindergarten again."

PARENTAL REDRESS?

As was mentioned earlier, parents have the legal right in some states to opt their children out of state testing. It would seem this may be a solution to prevent undue stress on one's child, but it can also be fraught with some serious consequences. There is no protection from the child being pressured by teachers and administrators to participate. There is no protection from parents being harassed by administrators to have their child tested—especially if the student is a "high scorer," which adds to the collective percent proficiency of both the teacher's classroom and the school. There is no protection from comments from other students about the one who opts out of testing.

We have never experienced ANY issues with opting him out of school until this year! I was called into school by the principal where they tried very hard to use guilt to get me to change my mind about the test, going so far as crying and saying that my son was feeling left out of the class, as if I was a poor parent that did not notice the pain of my child for my own cause. They stated that they were looking at teacher and funding sanctions primarily due to my choice to opt my son out of this test. I know that they were able to guilt the other two parents who opted their children out of the test (one for medical reasons) to allow their children to take the test. Those two children did take the test. People need to be aware of the way our children are being treated.[14]

SANCTIONS' MISINFORMATION

Coupled with this, under current NCLB guidelines, if a school does not have a 95 percent participation rate in state testing, it can be designated as a PI (program improvement school) and subject to sanctions. Also, beside the federal requirement, some states have their own assessment program that requires a minimum participation rate. California has an 85 percent participation rate requirement in order for the school to have a valid Academic Performance Index (API) score.

Parents who exercise their legal right to opt their child(ren) out of testing at a school site will contribute to lowering the participation rate because of their child(ren)'s lack of test scores being called "invalid." If a school has less than 85 percent participation rate, it is labeled as a "failing school." While parents are often told that their school will lose money as a result of these designations, it is blatant misinformation. There is nothing in either state or federal law that could remove either state funds or Title I moneys from the school as a result of poor test participation.

On February 25, 2004, California Schools Chief Jack O'Connell announced proposed changes to California's NCLB Accountability Workbook:

> I want to remove the penalty against schools where parents do not want their children to participate in state testing. It concerns me that the Bush Administration apparently does not support the rights of parents in this regard, because NCLB unfairly penalizes those schools where parents exempt their children from testing.[15]

Federal regulators did not agree, and so the law and its sanctions for less than 95 percent participation remain.

OPTING OUT RATIONALE

While parents may be able to opt their children out of testing in some states, they cannot opt them out of the approximately 175 days of teaching that supports the high-stakes testing mania unless they remove them from public school and enroll them in private schools, which are not subject to NCLB. The short-term harm to children is in the stress and angst of taking a battery of state, district, and local tests in many cases covering approximately two weeks of schooling. The long-term effects are the other thirty-four weeks of educational class time filled with strategies that focus almost entirely on test preparation in content and form.

This pollutes our students' desire for genuine lifelong learning and substitutes superficial goals based on test score acquisition. Opting out is a parent's way of not only protecting their child from the testing insanity but also protesting the high-stakes testing atmosphere that drives the curriculum.

> When district—or state-mandated testing comes around in our children's public schools, we opt out. We inform our kids' teachers and principal in writing that we do not want our children taking the tests. Each year, for the past six years, our requests have been respectfully accommodated. . . . When it comes to testing mandates, we exercise our rights as parents to protect our children from activities not in their interests. . . . We are not against standards. We support the kinds of student assessment needed to make sound educational decisions within a classroom.
>
> We believe every child can be challenged to exceed his or her own expectations. We are compelled to speak out, however, when parents and community members are led to believe that the best way to address these issues is for children to prepare for and complete hours of mandated testing. Our job as parents, as we see it, is to insist that community leaders respond thoughtfully to failures and dilemmas in schools—in ways that avoid oversimplification. We withdraw our support from practices that expect children to pay the price for improving public confidence in schools. That's why we opt out—to preserve the best of what public schools have to offer our kids.[16]

Some parents are willing to opt their children out of testing. They are aware that this decision contributes to lowering the participation rate below 95 percent. Even though it is possible that the school and district may suffer the sanctions associated with being a program improvement school, opting out is one way of protesting the testing regimen and protecting their child from its implementation. While districts are required to test as many of their students as possible, they are not required by state or federal law to prepare them for the testing. It is the fear of sanctions connected to low scores that drives them.

CARELESS SYSTEM

The desire to prepare for the testing is a local decision based on the drive to acquire high scores in order to avoid sanctions by both the state and federal laws. Once again, the educational mandate to enhance student learning is not focused on individual student need, but test score acquisition. The system is not concerned about caring for students. The system cannot show compassion. People do. Most districts do not have the confidence and courage to use best teaching and learning practices in the classroom regardless of the test score results.

The fear of poor scores becomes the reason to teach, and the reason to teach in a way that bears the hope of high scores, not of deeper learning and student interest. The system is attempting to sell the educational souls of our children and teachers in exchange for freedom from punishment.

TEACHER MARTYRS

Martyr is a Greek word that means "one who witnesses." They are witnesses to a belief or value that they hold dear and are willing to sacrifice to uphold. There are martyrs in this almost silent educational mayhem. This is the teachers' dilemma: Are they first and foremost a district employee, required to do whatever is asked of them, even if they know they are doing harm, or is their professional and ethical commitment to their students the ultimate guide?

What is the boundary between being a good employee and being a good teacher?

Where should a teacher's allegiances lie? There are those students, parents, and teachers who are willing to risk their comfort, security, and well-being for the sake of freedom from the tyranny of high-stakes testing and all its repercussions. When many teachers witness and experience the atrocities that fuel the educational genocide of so many of our students, some are willing to say, "No more!"

> Essential to societies we consider "free" is the right and responsibility to engage in civil disobedience, that is, to follow the dictates of one's conscience in nonviolent ways when called upon to do so. When our conscience is stirred professionally, though, we are summoned to an even higher standard: We are obliged to act. For educators, the essence of professional identity is the obligation to protect our students, not only from bullets or brutality, as we have seen teachers do regularly, but also from psychological and educational vandalism against their spirits. Part of this identity is also to protect the primacy of the teacher-student relationship.[17]

Here is a litany of a few of the educators who were willing to risk their livelihood for the love of kids:

> A Fresno Unified School District teacher has been suspended for five days because he refused to give a state-mandated standardized reading test, the Stanford

9, to his non-English-speaking pupils. The teacher, Silvio Manno, 43, said he thought that giving the test to his second graders at Rowell Elementary School here would have been "a humiliating insult" and ultimately harmful to them.[18]

A middle-school teacher in Greeley said Friday that he refuses to administer the Colorado Student Assessment Program tests to his students because they clash with his beliefs as an educator. This is the first time a teacher has refused to administer the tests, officials believe. State law requires teachers to give the exams, a fact that hasn't escaped Donald Perl, 58. "I've anguished over this for a long time, and I cannot administer these tests, knowing the population here and seeing how discriminatory the test is," said Perl, a Greeley resident who teaches eighth-grade Spanish, reading, and language arts at John Evans Middle School. . . . Perl said he is prepared to face the consequences of his refusal.[19]

Carl Chew, a 60-year-old sixth grade science teacher from Seattle, wrestled annually with his conscience about administering the Washington Assessment of Student Learning (WASL) tests to his students. "Each year I would give the WASL, and I would promise myself I would never do it again," he said. "I decided, 'I'm not going to wimp out this time.'" His refusal resulted in a nine-day unpaid suspension along with accolades from parents and teachers around the nation.

Chew explained his reasons in a *Seattle Post Intelligencer* commentary: "I performed this single act of civil disobedience based on personal moral and ethical grounds, as well as professional duty. I believe that the WASL is destructive to our children, teachers, schools, and parents. . . . I understand that my action has caused people pain, and I am truly sorry for that, but I could no longer stand idly by as something as wrong as the WASL is perpetrated on our children year after year." . . .

North Carolina special education teacher Doug Ward could no longer bring himself to give the state's alternative assessments to his students with severe disabilities. He was fired for his act of civil disobedience this spring. Ward, who had been teaching special needs students for three years, said he did not want to give a test to his students that was invalid and that they could not pass. "Someone needs to use a little common sense and say, 'I am just not going to do it,'" Ward said.

Like Chew, Ward has received support from parents, colleagues, and the community. Bob Williams, whose son Kyle was taught by Ward, said he admires his son's teacher for what he did, and that the test doesn't measure what Kyle has learned. "If you ask me as a parent is (Kyle) succeeding, you are darn right he is succeeding," Williams said. "When he started third grade, he couldn't walk down the hall. When he started school as a kindergartner, he was in a wheelchair. Now he can walk down the hall on his own. The test doesn't test that." . . .

St. Lucie County, Florida, high school Assistant Principal Teri Pinney resigned from her position in June rather than comply with her principal's request that she suspend students for sleeping or "Christmas Treeing" (filling in bubbles to make a pattern) during state testing and other requests she believes were unethical. Neither Pinney nor another assistant principal complied, but the principal suspended the students. Pinney said, "Two of the kids he suspended were good students, never got in trouble, and had excellent attendance. They were children of migrant Mexican workers. The parents pleaded with me and I gave in and lifted the suspensions. Of course, that opposition with my boss got me in trouble." In a newspaper commentary, Pinney expressed her dismay at the role played by testing in schools today: "I believe that misuse or overuse of standardized testing is creating a maddening race for everybody to that elusive finishing line." Pinney is now working with the Florida Coalition for Assessment Reform (FCAR) to build support for overhauling the state's controversial testing system.[20]

What is even more amazing is the fact that some students are themselves willing to stand up for their values and protest the harm high-stakes testing is having on them and their peers.

Macario Guajardo was one child left behind Wednesday when his classmates took the all-important Texas statewide reading test for promotion to the sixth grade. Actually, 11-year-old Macario, an unlikely crusader at 4-foot-11 and 93 pounds, wearing a Spider-Man T-shirt, left himself behind. He stayed out of school in protest against what he called "the big deal" of the testing program, which he said "keeps kids from expressing their imagination." "I don't think I'm brave," Macario said at his home here in the Rio Grande Valley.

"Any kid could do this. It does take a little bit of guts." . . . "The protests are very significant; I just think they're nearing the breaking point," said Angela Valenzuela, an associate professor of curriculum and instruction at the University of Texas and the editor of a collection of critical essays, "Leaving Children Behind," published recently by the State University of New York Press. . . .

In San Antonio on Tuesday, a 14-year-old high school freshman, Mia Kang, refused to take the required reading test, known as the TAKS, for Texas Assessment of Knowledge and Skills. Two years ago, another San Antonio freshman, Kimberly Marciniak, 15, made headlines when she boycotted the same reading test in its debut year. . . . Also in 2003, two Washington State high school sophomores refused to take that state's mandatory exams. In 2002, parents in Scarsdale, N.Y., organized a boycott of the eighth-grade test. . . .

And in Stewart, Ohio, a high school senior, John Wood, 17, who has refused to take any statewide test since the seventh grade, has lost out on graduating this spring. That poses a quandary for his father, George, who is coeditor of *Many Children Left Behind*, a 2004 book critical of the federal law, but is also principal of John's school and must keep him from graduating. George Wood said he supported his son, who has been accepted by two private colleges.[21]

CARE FOR STUDENTS REDEEMS

So why do so many educators have their protective hackles up on this issue? We love our students. We care for both their short- and long-term educational well-being. Students were not created for schools to prosper; rather, schools were created for students to prosper. We believe in children's individual uniqueness and their desire to know the world about them.

Even if some parents can't see what is happening to their children, we can. We would be less than professional if we did not make every effort to inform and reveal the heart of the high-stakes testing mania in the hope that parents would be on the forefront of change for their children. Care for our students is what will redeem our classrooms. Educators and parents are being called to free our students from distress and harm. When we see a physical fight between two people and recognize that one or both are in danger of serious harm, we are called to do what we can to stop the beating or call for help.

We must attempt to stop the violence before we can facilitate reconciliation. Our students are captives in a system that is killing their desire to be lifelong learners. We first must stop the beating. It is the care and concern for students that will propel us to that end. As I heard Ray Romano say in his sitcom *Everybody Loves Raymond* while speaking to his children's school board, "We are so concerned about students' future in the global economy that we take away their present."

10

No Excuses, Just Results

I was sitting in the biology classroom waiting for class to start. I was observing my student teacher get ready to teach a lesson. In walked about a dozen AVID (Advancement Via Individual Determination) students. AVID is a program designed to help underachieving middle and high school students prepare for and succeed in college.

Each student wore a black sweatshirt. On the back in white letters was emblazoned—NO EXCUSES, JUST RESULTS. The night before I had just begun to read Susan Ohanian's *When Childhood Collides with NCLB*.

> Don't try to blame Poverty
> Instead, tattoo *No Excuses* on your soul.
> Repeat that to third graders:
> *No Excuses, No Excuses, No Excuses . . .*
> Education reporters
> Repeat the corporate politico mantra
> *"No excuses!"*
> Deaf to pleading
> Deaf to explanations
> Deaf to research
> *. . . Alert to big money*
> Deaf to poverty's tears.[1]

— Susan Ohanian

EXCUSES IN BUSINESS

In the *St. Louis Business Journal*, I read this article by Greta Schulz, president and CEO of Pro Active Training and Consulting:

> Economic Uncertainty or Excuse-Making?
> Don't fall victim to a salesperson's belief that "people are spending less" and "it's an election year." Excuses, excuses, excuses! If all sales people aren't strong enough to make it through tough times, they probably don't belong on your team. . . . Neither our mortgage lender, our bank nor the power company will accept the excuse of the economy for non-payment. Why should we? Now is when the real sales professionals can shine.[2]

When on the Internet researching on how to start an online business, I found the following:

> Start an Internet Business. How to Make a Start in Business without Making Excuses: Scared to Start an Internet Business for Yourself? Excuses Are for the Weak![3]

STATES, DISTRICTS, SCHOOLS, AND EXCUSES

The state of Kentucky has made it clear that excuses are not part of their educational policy:

> Not only is it a moral imperative, reducing the achievement gap is a necessity if ALL schools and ALL students are to reach proficiency by 2014. In Kentucky there can be NO EXCUSES for failure, only reasons for student success in our public schools. NO EXCUSES, JUST RESULTS.
> "We can whenever and wherever we choose successfully teach all children whose schooling is of interest to us. We already know more than we need in order to do this. Whether we do must finally depend on how we feel about the fact that we haven't so far."[4]

In California:

> Hollingworth Elementary Launches College Program—Becomes First "No Excuses University" School in San Gabriel Valley.[5]

So does Greenway elementary school in Arizona:

A no-excuses approach to school improvement in Bisbee, Arizona: At Green-way, however, accepting mediocrity is not an option. When it comes to student learning, "we have active control, six hours a day, five days a week, for 180 days a year," says Principal John Taylor. "We can offer no excuses."[6]

And even former President Bush weighs in on educational excuses at a Small Business Roundtable speech:

And if we spend federal money, particularly on disadvantaged children, the debate ought to be not whether or not we ought to spend money on disadvantaged children; the debate ought to be, are we getting our money's worth?

I believe every child can learn. I refuse to accept excuses that there are certain children who can't learn; therefore, let's don't measure or let's just move them through the system.[7]

EXCUSES ARE BOTHERSOME

An excuse often carries with it a negative implication, a cop-out. Most of the time an excuse is interpreted as an alibi, as deceitful, and masking or escaping responsibility. We make an excuse acceptable when we place more positive descriptors in front of it—like the phrases "a justifiable excuse," "a plausible excuse," "an approved excuse," and "an understandable excuse."

Excuses are assuaged when understood and accepted as being true. They can be painful and alienating when believed to be contrived—when we have an expectation of a specific type of behavior and then someone says, "I can't do that," "I can't come to the party, I am sick," or "I can't help you move if it involves heavy lifting. I have a bad back." Many of us have problems acknowledging the truth of their claim.

An excuse is a reason for noncompliance. A person offering an excuse may be asking to be believed, or to be forgiven, or to be accepted, or possibly all three. It is hoped that the excuse can be transformed into a justifiable explanation without penalty. The recipient of an excuse is at a moment of challenge to their values. How has the world (family, friends, respected professionals, and others) responded to my excuses? Do I follow one or more of their patterns of excuse reaction? In my life's work have I been trained how to deal with excuses? Do I concur or do I question? Each of us must decide for ourselves where we stand on the idea of excuses.

One type of response is to give the benefit of any doubt to the person offering an excuse, thinking, "Until shown that there is good reason to not believe a person, I will consider them trustworthy and accept their excuses as valid." The polar opposite is to disbelieve all excuses: "There is no good reason to believe any excuse. I will consider no excuse trustworthy and accept none."

This form of outright rejection (whether or not an explanation is offered as justification) says, "I do not accept or give excuses. I do not have the willingness and/or the capacity to even listen to an excuse—even one within me." Being open to hear the excuse of the person seeking acceptance takes time and energy. Refusal to listen can indicate that this person believes that they have imagined all possible explanations and that none are satisfactory. The fallacy with this type of thinking is that it is not even possible for humans to think of infinity, much less think of an infinite set of explanations and reject each one. So there has to be more to this than just that.

ACCEPTING EXCUSES

Unwillingness to listen is just a smokescreen. Those who reject all excuses are afraid of their own capacity to forgive and the possible results. Once compassion has been extended and accepted, the fear is that others will ask for this mercy too. To those for whom "No Excuses" is their mantra, the consequences of acceptance are so threatening that one dare not even consider that option. So they make the decision that there will be no excuses, no forgiveness, and no acceptance—no matter what.

> Presenting a deliberately flawed version of reality, fearing that the truth will lead to excuses, is not only corrupt but also self-defeating. . . . Instead, however, critical voices for reform have been silenced, told they should stick to their knitting, fearing an accusation that denouncing inequality is tantamount to "making excuses."[8]

When one opens oneself up to the possibility of accepting excuses, one result may be that the desired effect does not come to pass. Think of a sales manager who sets quotas for each of his salespersons. Why quotas? Because the sales manager is also under the scrutiny of his supervisor, who has expectations of a certain amount of profit.

The sales manager believes his salary and/or his job will be at stake if these expectations do not come to pass. Sure enough, one of his salespersons does not make the quota, using the "excuse" that there is a downturn in the economy and vendors are reluctant to buy. The sales manager does not want to consider a world containing failure. He fears that accepting the excuse as valid will support the possibility of no future successes. So he may choose to sanitize his world from failure by firing that salesman and demonstrating his high expectations to his superiors.

FAILURE IS NATURAL

The "no excuses" folks know little of how human progress has been made over the millennia. Civilizations, cultures, and individuals have accepted failure as their companion. How frequently does a baby have to fall before it learns to walk? How many failures can it endure?

Each reiteration brings on a slightly modified strategy. Is the spirit daunted? Does the baby just give up? Do the parents? On some level, both know that success will come and that sufficient failure is needed for walking to take place. The parents know that walking is a natural process. There is no need for punishment to arrive at the desired results. If the baby could talk, all excuses would be accepted. Persistence will pay off.

FAILURES AND SUCCESS

I once took my five children to a local lake, which had a rocky shoreline. No sooner than they had exited the van did they run to the lake's edge. There was a buoy about thirty yards from shore. For over an hour they picked up various size stones and tried to hit the buoy. They rarely did. But they persisted. When they came in for lunch I told them that I was impressed with their desire to hit the buoy and asked them why they were doing it. Their unanimous answer: "It was fun!" None offered an "excuse" for missing, nor did I suggest any. I told them I would like to join them at the shore's edge after lunch and record their hits and misses.

They did not want me to do that. They told me it would take all the fun out of it. You see, they had accepted misses as part of their rock-throwing process. Every throw had an excuse for missing but none was expected and none was given. They rejoiced whenever they got a hit.

Nearly every night before we go off to bed, my wife and I play a couple of hands of solitaire. We have three types that we normally play. It is rare that we win but when we do we slap hands and get a thrill out of it. Professional baseball players like to get some kind of a base hit. Even the best of players rarely bats near .400 for a season. That is to say, most of the time a batter strikes out.

A good hitter batting .300 strikes out 70 percent of the time, with a hit only 30 percent of the time. Excuses could abound: "I was fooled." "I swung too soon." "I swung too late." There is a lot of failure in baseball. Why do they still keep coming up to the plate? Each time at bat players have another opportunity to have learned from their mistakes and improve. They have accepted failure as part of the batting process. The reasons for failure, their excuses, become the motivation for progress. It is part of the game, according to Michael Jordan:

> I've missed more than 9,000 shots in my career. I've lost more than 300 games, and 26 times I've been trusted to take the game winning shot and missed. Throughout my life and career I've failed and failed and failed again. And, that's why I succeed.[9]

USE EXCUSES

We have not learned this in the game of business or in the game of education. We have made excuses an enemy rather than a friend. Wouldn't it be great to hear a teacher say to a student, "Great mistake! What is your excuse? Do you see what you did wrong? Do you know what to do if you see this again? OK, now go and give it another try." While this may be the desire on the part of many teachers, their site and district practices and policies may not encourage taking advantage of student mistakes and excuses as a pedagogical tool.

The "no excuses, just results" folks do not understand the human condition. Each invention that has advanced civilization has done so on the back of excuses. Faulty reasoning, design, and construction have plagued human progress since our beginnings. Each excuse became a stepping stone to the next version of buildings, airplanes, and so many other discoveries.

The point is not that we have excuses, but what do we do with them? How do excuses advance our cause?

> Charles F. Kettering of General Motors once said, "I think it was the Brookings Institution that made a study that said the more educated you were the less likely you were to become an inventor. The reason why is: From the time a kid

starts kindergarten to the time he graduates from college he will be examined two or three or four times a year and if he flunks one, he's out. Now an inventor fails 999 times, and if he succeeds once he's in. An inventor treats his failures as practice shots."[10]

In 1978, James Dyson noticed how the air filter in the Ballbarrow spray-finishing room was constantly clogging with powder particles. So he designed and built an industrial cyclone tower, which removed the powder particles. Could the same principle work in a vacuum cleaner? Five years and 5,127 prototypes later, the world's first bagless vacuum cleaner from Dyson arrived.

RECORDING EXCUSES?

Schooling has made it a practice of recording successes and failures and ignoring excuses. We record those successes and failures as grades and scores. We keep track of them. But it is precisely the excuses for our successes and failures that take us down the path of growth. That's right—you can have an excuse for an apparent success.

I cannot tell you how often I would have students come to the correct conclusion from erroneous thinking. A correct answer seems to be a success, but, when you ask the student for justification, their explanation may not hold water. When we summarize a student's learning with grades and scores, we neglect the most telling part of their story: How did they progress from mistakes and excuses to understanding and mastery of the concepts? "How they did it" is more telling than the end result.

PUSH OUTS

High-stakes testing supporters have not trained themselves to listen to another's excuses. They may relegate that to the work of a psychologist. They say that they are all "business." Freely translated, it says that they do not want to spend the time, or make the time, to assess how students move from their excuses to personal progress.

The fact is that the "no excuse" high-stakes testing supporters care less about a student as a person, but more about what that student's scores can do for them. They would eliminate students who cannot produce the scores they want when they want them. This is no different from business managers who eliminate salespersons from their team because they cannot produce what they want and when they want it. How acceptable could low-scoring students be to a school or district?

> As a result, we find administrators and teachers doing things that they themselves find reprehensible. We are test-prepping our kids into the dropout line (fewer than one-half of minorities nationwide are graduating). School is becoming irrelevant. Research is clear on what motivates kids to engage in schoolwork. Children want to be loved by their teacher, to be respected for who they are and to feel that their skills and talents will contribute to society's improvement. . . . It's time to scrap high-stakes tests and use ethical, responsible, sensible, motivational means that actually connect and reach our children. Failure to do so will continue to push students out of school into the streets or to prisons.[11]

CARING FORGIVES

"No excuses, just results" people are afraid of changing views and reexamining values—namely, that people are more important than their high-stakes test agenda. Forgiveness and compassion may not have been a significant part of their personal development, but in order to participate in education, both must become learned skills. Forgiveness and compassion have their source in care and concern for others' well-being.

A system cannot show this care and concern. Only people can. It is action taken either when you do or do not feel like it. It is doing the good for oneself and others. Embracing excuses is embracing the human condition. It acknowledges faults and failings as a path to growth. Caring extends forgiveness and compassion as acknowledgement of our personal excuses and failings and gives hope.

This awareness is reflected in the writings of many respected leaders:

> "The weak can never forgive. Forgiveness is the attribute of the strong." —Gandhi

> "The more I can love the world, the sooner I shall be able to forgive the world." —Sri Chinmoy

> "If we really want to love, we must learn how to forgive." —Mother Teresa of Calcutta

"We must develop and maintain the capacity to forgive. He who is devoid of the power to forgive is devoid of the power to love." —Martin Luther King Jr.

"What power has love but forgiveness?" —William Carlos Williams

[If my brother keeps on sinning against me, how many times do I have to forgive him? Seven times?] "Not seven times, but seventy times seven." —Jesus of Nazareth

NONFORGIVING WORLD?

Educators play a key role in helping to shape the future of our society by mentoring its youth. We give examples of the way we hope the world will be. We try to live our values in our interactions with our students. We not only teach them things *about* the world, in that we instruct skills and knowledge, but also, and more important, we help develop an attitude *toward* the world, self, and others.

It is in and through the student-teacher relationship that the desire for lifelong learning can be fostered. A classroom that does not permit excuses is one that does not permit engagement of a full person. All humans err. All students have excuses for their faults—some valid, some contrived. But in both cases, it is the teacher who can make those excuses into learning experiences. Having a "no excuses, just results" mindset teaches students that what is best is an unforgiving world; one in which compassion and forgiveness are weaknesses, not strengths.

There is a story of a contractor who was on the brink of bankruptcy. In speaking before the judge he asked for more time to make his payments to his creditors. Even though there was scant legal precedent for his decision, the judge was so moved by his pleadings that he permitted a time extension for payment.

No sooner had the contractor left the courtroom than he came upon one of his clients who was at the courthouse on another matter. He told the client that he needed to be paid so he could in turn pay his creditors. The client asked for patience, as he was just starting back to work. The contractor would not listen to his excuse and went right to the appropriate office to have his client's wages garnered and a lien put on his home. This story says that although most of us would like our mistakes forgiven, it is often very difficult to forgive another's excuses.

In part of his talk to the Business Roundtable, cited above, President Bush said, "I refuse to accept excuses that there are certain children who can't learn." Teacher Glenda Puett has a different worldview:

State testing.
"learning disabled"
Twelve year olds
Drumming fingers,
Panicked eyes searching,
Squinting,
Hoping concentrating on shapes of letters
Will bring eurekas to their confusion.
Squeezing foreheads
As if answers will ooze through their arms
To tools
Of pencils ready and oh so willing to answer
Questions.
Questions which reflect paragraphs
Made of words, mysterious symbols
Created to measure the worth of a twelve year old mind
If only reading were possible.
State testing.
"Learning disabled"
twelve year old terrified to admit
His confusion.
Two hours trying to
Fill in bubbles slowly
As if to make the effort would create success.
Each minute sinking deeper into
The despair of self-loathing.
The garble on the pages pointing their
Defiant arrows toward his inward
Feeling of stupidity
If only he could read.
Testing
"learning disabled"
Reading . . .
Like everything would come together
If effort prevailed.
Twelve year olds
Teachers

Parents
Even the president says it's possible.
Too bad
That touted belief
Couldn't heal
The helplessness
In twelve year olds' eyes.[12]

What kind of world are we forming when we trumpet, "no excuses, just results"? We need to reinvent our classrooms, schools, and districts to accept the reality of mistakes, errors, and excuses, and build on the processes of student learning through persistence and forgiveness.

Love Truth but pardon Error

—*Voltaire*

11

Forgiving Learning

So what are we to do? If high-stakes testing and all its attendant baggage were to disappear, how could we assess what students know and are able to do? How are we to modify the way in which our classrooms are structured to fit brain-compatible learning? What are the lessons that our experiences with the emphasis on high-stakes testing have taught us?

HIGH-STAKES TESTING LESSONS LEARNED

A synopsis:

High-stakes test score results are not measures of any aspects of education. They do not tell the truth about what a student knows and is able to do or about the effectiveness of teachers and the quality of schools and districts.

- Some who espouse the high-stakes testing mantra have an obsession with numbers and quantification, believing that every meaningful aspect of the human endeavor can be measured.
- The intense focus on test preparation and the testing itself produces both short- and long-term harm to the physical, psychological, and educational health of children.
- The focus on testing diminishes students' desire to become lifelong learners and substitutes a false image of their accomplishments.

- The high-stakes testing system does not care about the impact on individual students but rather on their ability to produce numerical data, no matter how flawed.
- The use of misinformation, fear, threats, and intimidation are the medium by which this system is maintained.
- Those who initiated and continue to promulgate this educational genocide are predominantly business and cooperating governmental agencies whose quest for financial gain and fear of corporate competition enlist public schools as training grounds for their pool of workers.

EDUCATION'S TRUE GOALS

These lessons learned fly in the face of the uniqueness of each student and their personal hopes, dreams, and aspirations. Each student comes to us with the free will to choose his or her direction in life. Education's goal is to provide options, skills, values, discipline, and knowledge sufficient at each student's level of maturation to make good choices in contributing to his or her individual and societal growth.

We are not here to decide for the student where they should go in life. Public school educators are not working for the good of business, government, education, military, social services, religious institutions, or any other affiliation or group with its own motives and goals. We are working for students. We believe that students will have the opportunities to align themselves at various times in their lives to one or more personal callings.

We are not here to prepare them exclusively for competition in the global marketplace. They may not want to compete in any marketplace. We hope that they will make good choices for the betterment of themselves, the community in which they live, and our country. That is what freedom is all about.

STUDENTS ARE POTENTIAL

This then should be the foundation of each classroom, not with a lockstep one-size-fits-all approach to classroom learning. We must look upon each student as potential. Each school experience should be orchestrated by adults to accept students as they come to us, and, within our areas of expertise to instruct, to nurture them.

Usually, we know little of the extent of each student's prior experiences in life outside school. But one thing we do know is that they come to us with an organ for learning: the brain. This brain has acquired many skills and much knowledge outside formal schooling. These experiences have been mostly random, not sequential. At one moment, students learn how to hit a baseball, at another how to read a comic book, and again how to program the DVD/VCR/TiVo, send and receive text messages on their cell phones, and escape dangerous situations.

The human condition has always been that we err. We have evolved by learning from our mistakes. This is a natural part of what it means to be human. Our brain uses these errors to its advantage. Babies who are learning how to walk, and continue to forgive themselves each time they fall, or baseball players who forgive themselves each time they make an out, learn from their failings.

BRAIN-COMPATIBLE LEARNING

To develop a classroom culture that best suits our students, we must then know how to maximize the potential for brain-compatible learning. It should be the goal of every district, school, classroom, and teacher to develop and encourage a brain-friendly environment.

A teacher needs to know that the brain learns best when it is fed and healthy and free from threat. A hungry brain will want to seek food before learning. A threatened brain will seek protection before participation in classroom activities. The brain learns best when levels of fear and threat are reduced.

While it is the responsibility of the school and district to provide a safe environment, food/health services, and shelter, teachers must so design their classrooms with practices, policies, and procedures that personalize the key brain needs that are within their purview. If the neocortex does not have its needs met, it "downshifts" to either or both the reptilian brain and old mammalian brain to seek its requirements before being open to learning. A student may "tune out" when not feeling well. Another student may "cut class" to hang out with friends when not feeling accepted in a classroom or school.

For the most part, teachers are not in control of what students bring into the classroom, but they can have some measure of confidence with brain-compatible structures and procedures they establish for their students. Neocortex functioning is at a minimum when schooling fears are not dealt with. It will never be possible to eliminate all of these fears, but they can be reduced.

From over thirty years of student observations and discussions I have found four distinct classroom fears: fear of the teacher, fear of other students, fear of the difficulty of the course or grade-level content, and fear of their grades/scores. "Forgiving learning" is what happens when these apprehensions are transformed in a brain-compatible way. Forgiving learning is predicated on the reduction of student educational fears with conversion to confidence and hope. This process can begin in the classroom, be supported by the school site, and nurtured by the district.

FEAR OF THE TEACHER

A teacher is a new person in the student's life, one that students will have to be involved with on a regular basis for over nine months. Are the teachers nice or mean? Are there smiles or frowns? Do students sense that their teachers like them and enjoy being around kids? How do students feel around their teachers when they hear them speak and interact with others and themselves? From the beginning, the student's old mammalian brain is discerning the relational atmosphere with this new and important person. For the most part, teachers and students are assigned to each other rather than choosing one another. What type of future does the student foresee with them?

Students sometimes think, "When I interact with my teachers do I sense that they will be on my side or will they be adversaries? Do I find myself intimidated and on the defensive? Will this teacher be someone I will have to 'get through' or will they be supportive and encouraging?" The concern and anticipation can wax and wane with the initial contacts until the student decides what the nature of the relationship will be and the degree of fear that must be dealt with. How can the teacher minimize or reduce this possible anxiety?

My Story

It was the early 1980s (I began teaching in 1966), and I was teaching high school physics. From their nonverbal cues as well as their conversations, I became aware that many of my students saw me and many of their other teachers as adversaries in their daily school life. Instructors were not only seen as authority figures but were like classroom obstacles that had to be "dealt with" in order to be successful.

How I related to my students was going to, in a large measure, determine whether they had a hopeful or despairing outlook on the whole school year in my class. Over the first fourteen years of my teaching, I was becoming more and more frustrated with the kind of relationships I had with my students. I wanted to do something different. To decide how I was going to approach them I asked myself this question: "With whom in my own schooling was I most hopeful about the upcoming year?" It came to me in a flash: my high school athletic coaches. No matter what sport I went out for, the clear message was that they were for me.

I knew they were going to make me work hard, but I had the sense to know that it was going to be for my good, the good of the team, and the pride of the school. My coaches were on my side. So I decided to do an experiment. What would happen if I tried to carry this model into my classroom? All I knew was that my coaches seemed to have a way of doing things that was significantly different from what I had experienced in my regular classes. I wanted somehow to translate this coaching mentality into my teaching and see what happened.

Coach?

I began by doing some research into the word *coach*. Much to my surprise, I found that the word originated from a small village in Hungary called Kocs. This village became quite famous in the 1450s for building "Cinderella"-type carriages. These carriages were soon called *coche* (Fr.), since they came from Kocs (pronounced "coach"). As medieval universities began to develop, its instructors were sometimes called *coaches* (Eng.) by their students since they "carried them along" in the fashion of a carriage.

Well, well! So coaches were really teachers who carried along their students. To be carried along academically by one's instructor is a fairly personal event exemplified by the nurturing and encouraging behavior of the "coach." Historically, a later evolving approach to university instruction were those teachers who, rather than "coaching" their students, stood before their classes and espoused or "professed" what they knew to them—professors. It seems that with the birth of the industrial and scientific revolutions beginning in the 1800s, teachers became more associated with the latter rather than teachers who "coached" their students.

But instead of dying, the concept of coaching took on a firm root in athletic events, apparently lacking the sophistication to be worthy of the scientific and industrial approach to schooling. So coaches did for athletics what professors were supposed to do for academics.

An Adversary

In surveying many middle and high school students, there was an over-whelming consensus that when they walk into a new classroom, they anticipate that the teacher may be a type of enemy, someone they will have to conquer or get through. All too frequently, students' first impressions are born out in the reality of the atmospheres and structures of their past classrooms. So I asked myself: How could I begin to change this perception?

I asked myself what I wanted to be called. What's in a name? In this case, a lot. At the beginning of the school year, I ask them to either call me Coach or Coach Lucido. I tell them that I want them to see me as their mentor, as a person in their corner to support, encourage, and direct their learning. I want them to perceive me as they would expect to see any good coach: knowledgeable, experienced, enthusiastic, and, most important, interested in each of them as individuals on a path of lifelong learning.

This starts them thinking, "What is this all about? Is this just a change in name only or will things really be different in here than a regular classroom, and if so, in what ways?" Coaching in its present-day usage implies being for the athlete. It is the athlete and the coach who engage in a mutual endeavor to ensure that the athlete continues to improve in the sport. Athletes *assume* that their coaches will be on their side and that coaches want them to improve. The bottom line is that my students really need to believe that I will be on their side.

In order to begin this process of academic coaching, I had to change the way they saw me. I wanted to shake their old mentality and have them look at their teacher through new eyes. Whether in the classroom or in the hallway, when they addressed me as "coach," I sensed a new and healthy sense of camaraderie. It has made inroads into their fear of the teacher.

For elementary students, their closeness and trust of their parents/responsible adults often become transferred to their teachers. They expect their teachers to care about them and to have their welfare as a top priority. Whether elementary, middle school, or high school, the coaching mindset is a healthy way to approach one's relationship with students. With this change I have found students to be much more vulnerable and willing to share what is going on in their lives that might be affecting their connection with learning.

Being an academic coach has put me on the same side of the court or playing field as my students. I am less their adversary. They are not alone in their desire to be successful. I am seen now as in their corner, doing what I can to help them begin to fulfill their dreams.

At the Heart

In today's ordinary classroom, a course of study is designed so that it can be completed in a set number of days. With high-stakes testing as the driver, the focus of many classroom activities is "covering" state teaching standards. Often, the lessons are artificially paced so that each is taught in sequence at a specified rate regardless of student comprehension.

In many cases, the lessons are scripted for the teachers to follow line by line so that content completion corresponds to district benchmark and state testing calendars. The tests become the central concern around which classroom sessions are planned. In this high-stakes testing milieu, many teachers ask the question, "How can I get through this many standards in this many days so the students will score high on the test(s)?"

In forgiving learning it is the student, not the testing, that is at the heart of planning each day's activities. The coach (teacher) asks a different question: "How can I organize this experience so that these students will be engaged and masterful learners of the course/grade level standards in my time with them?" Topic organization and process is centered on the clientele in the classroom, not testing requirements. How are these students coming to me? What are their strengths and weaknesses as individuals and as a group? What student differences need to be tended to within this context? With this background information, the coach is addressing the relational needs of the brain.

FEAR OF FELLOW STUDENTS

There is not just the teacher-student bond that provides a nurturing environment within the classroom. Brain-compatible learning requires reducing cultural, social, and academic fears among students. It is paramount that coaches want students to enjoy the classroom atmosphere where fear of other students, especially as competitors, can be minimized. Using a teaming structure can concretize students' getting to know the instructor and fellow students as helpful companions on this educational journey. Athletic coaches have teams and teams have coaches. Teams know that both the coach and fellow athletes have but one purpose: to be successful as individuals and as a unit.

Initial and ongoing team-building activities outside subject matter content establishes camaraderie and fraternity. Classroom exercises and activities utilizing students' learning styles, stereotypes, positive and negative criticism, thoughts versus feelings, opinions versus values, the importance of growing from mistakes, and affirming self and others set the tone for understanding and mutual respect.

These insights are coupled with processes for enhancing listening skills: body language, checking for understanding, and distinguishing hearing from listening. While this entire affective program takes place during the first few weeks of school, mini-reminders and related activities are established throughout the school year. This emphasizes the importance of healthy human relationships to learning and primes the neocortex for openness to course content by satisfying the needs of the old mammalian brain.

Cooperation, Not Competition

Some classrooms operate on the mentality of personal competition among students. This becomes obvious in the way grading curves are created, scores are announced or posted, grades and progress histograms are used, and praise of one or more student's high-stakes testing success are used to encourage students to compete with one another. This competitive mindset supports the frame of mind that "it's a dog-eat-dog world." It reinforces the view that others on this planet, fellow students included, are to be competed with rather than cooperated with.

Even as a student enters a classroom on the first day, he or she may think something like "Mary Sue Williams is in here. There goes my A!" Sometimes girls in math and science classes are afraid of the perceived advantage that boys have. Students of one culture known for their academic prowess are seen as competitors to students in another. Teaming can begin to alleviate the tensions based on this artificial rivalry.

Coaching in forgiving learning is dependent upon cooperation between team members, not competition. Learning how to speak a foreign language, learning how to write creatively, or calculating the area under a curve is difficult enough without the added anxiety of competing with the person sitting next to you. We all know that on athletic teams there *is* competition among team members for a place on the squad. This is because there are predefined numbers allowed on each team. In the classroom we do not suffer from this limitation: Everyone can be on the team! We can begin to develop the kind of cooperation and communication that is going to be required when they work with others in the real world.

Mitigation

Since the focus of the team is to help everyone reach his or her academic potential, then with the added mentorship of the coach, each student has a tremendous support system right in the classroom. Fears of the teacher as an adversary and other students as competitors become mitigated by the initial and ongoing activities and resulting enhanced relationships.

Learning then becomes a shared effort on the part of all. In the document *Project 2061—Science for all Americans*, the American Association for the Advancement of Science makes this quite clear:

> Use a team approach. The collaborative nature of scientific and technological work should be strongly reinforced by frequent group activity in the classroom. Scientists and engineers work mostly in groups and less often as isolated investigators. Similarly, students should gain experience sharing responsibility, for learning with each other. In the process of coming to common understandings, students in a group must frequently inform each other about procedures and meanings, argue over findings, and assess how the task is progressing. In the context of team responsibility, feedback and communication become more realistic and of a character very different from the usual individualistic textbook-homework-recitation approach.[1]

FEAR OF COURSE/GRADE LEVEL

With an effective plan in place on how to mitigate teacher-student and student-student anxieties, the next concern is to address student fears of the course or grade level. Much has been written about math anxiety and science anxiety, but researchers, parents, and teachers have also found students who exhibit elementary, middle, and high school anxieties.

> It's probably safe to say that there isn't anyone who doesn't think back on their school days without remembering times of anxiety. What we don't realize when we're going through it, of course, is that many of our peers are going through the same thing. Indeed, certain extraordinary school-related stresses seem to land on kids at predictable stages. In some cases, however, children may feel so

anxious about school or about what's going on in their lives that they develop a fear of school and even, in some cases, refuse to attend. If that happens, extra help is often needed.[2]

Upon entering a new classroom situation, some students are convinced by hearsay that their academic success is in doubt. Comments by other students, friends, and even parents that "third grade is difficult," "math is hard," or "English is boring" make some students' initial encounters with school learning challenging.

While there are always some difficulties to be overcome in learning anything new, students are much more willing to expend time and energy when the task at hand can be made *relevant* to their daily lives. Engaging new experiences that have personal meaning become more attractive and foster persistence. Have you ever tried to crawl on all fours for a few hours at a time? It hurts! Yet babies do it on rugs, hard floors, cement, dirt, and just about any other place. Babies are willing to put up with the pain because they have a greater desire to be mobile and explore their world.

The same can be said of some of those students who were "failures" in our K–12 schools but who become willing to endure the difficulties of re-entering school even when they may have families and full-time jobs. Why? Because the knowledge or skills they now want have become relevant—very important to their daily lives. Listen to music? Relevancy! Why do so many of our students dislike the classroom situation? It is not relevant to their daily lives.

Famed psychologist Carl Rogers similarly reports in *Freedom to Learn*:

> But nearly every student finds that large portions of his curriculum are for him, meaningless. Thus education becomes the futile attempt to learn material, which has no personal meaning.[3]

The Present

When I was a student, I just did what I was told to do with little sense of purpose except for being constantly told that I would need it for my future. When I became a teacher, I realized that planning for the future is important, but neither my students nor I lived there. We lived in the present. The future will be prepared for when the present has meaning. Therefore, when employing forgiving learning, a key challenge is to make what is being taught relevant to students in their everyday lives. Even if you teach a mandatory course, once relevance is established, what is required can soon become desired.

Here are a few examples: If I were to teach history, I would start with students' family trees. I could then go back to cultures and show how they affect who each of us is *now*. If I were to teach English, I would begin by teaching my students how to write good notes to other students in the class or text them with proper sentences, spelling, and punctuation. Writing notes and "texting" is what some of them already do, so teach all the rules of good grammar and reading using these relevant vehicles. In teaching science, use the chemistry of the foods they eat, the physics of the music they listen to, the television they watch, and computers they use. When students can see the relationships between their time at school and the real things in their daily experiences, their learning will stick, not in preparation for high-stakes testing, but for their personal lives.

Expand Relevancy

Relevance is reinforced when students can see that the topic being discussed also has meaning to their instructor. Our students can tell if we are enthusiastic and involved with the thought of them being as captivated with what we are teaching as we are. Isn't this what we see in good coaches? We observe a kind of single-mindedness that seems to want to draw the athlete into a degree of involvement in the sport that they have. A teacher's example is a very powerful testimony as to the value and importance of what they are doing.

FEAR OF GRADES

The last, yet most significant, anxiety to be addressed is the fear of report card grades. This fear is based on a perceived lack of control and the possible impact grades have on their relationship with their parent(s), school activities, insurance/driving licenses, graduation, employment, college acceptance, and the like. In the forgiving learning process, it begins with the classroom atmosphere the teacher establishes regarding grades.

When an athletic coach first meets with her team, she wants to let them know that her goal is for all athletes to be excellent in their role on the team. She would not say, "You know I want some of you to be excellent, some of you pretty good, most average, and a few of you poor along with some dropouts." A coach does not want a distribution curve of quality, but tries to create a program that is designed for all to become excellent.

Transformation

Imagine this happening to you: You are awaiting a much-anticipated flight to visit family and friends. You are chatting with others in line about the thrill you get when the plane takes off. Upon being greeted by the flight attendant and having your ticket taken, you randomly glance to your left and a pilot's certificate catches your eye. On a very professional form it says, "This is to certify that Captain John Jones has passed takeoffs with a C+, flying with a C, and landings with a D." You stop. A shudder goes through you. The cold hard reality hits home: "This guy hasn't mastered anything about flying this plane. I could die!"

How many of us would submit to open heart or brain surgery with a doctor who is average or barely "passed" the class? How many of us would have a home built by a contractor who was "mediocre" in his construction practices? This isn't the way we think. More often than not we assume that, within a range of accomplishment, those we employ to do something for us have achieved a basic mastery of those abilities. This is most often validated by association with one or more masters/journeyman of that profession as determined by their governing bodies.

Mistakes Are OK

Under the guidance of the master/journeyman, apprentices are given the freedom to make mistakes and then to learn from them so as to enhance their skills and knowledge. In order to free a student from the fear of grades and scores, the opportunity must be provided for a student to repeat assignments and assessments over and over without penalty. Each time they should receive directions from the coach as to what they did right, what they did wrong, and how to improve.

It does little good for a swimming coach to walk along the edge of the pool and yell "C+" . . . "B-" . . . "C". . . "A" . . . "D" as the swimmer strokes and kicks in her practice laps. To be effective and supportive, the coach must talk to her, saying things like "Dig your hands deeper in the water. Your kick is great. Cup your palms. Okay, now increase your pace." This must be the same protocol used on each assignment and assessment tool. If a student can be convinced that errors are to be expected and can be overcome with sufficient practice and without punishment, the resulting effort will prove that their persistence does make a difference.

If you have ever listened to a coach speaking to an athlete, you typically can pick up a number of distinct elements: "Adrienne, that was a pretty good dive, but your feet came apart just as you hit the water. Go up and give it another try and this time keep those toes pointed." The first and most obvious observation is that the coach used words, not abstract symbols, to communicate with Adrienne.

Notice what the coach did in the comment to Adrienne. He gave a personal ("Adrienne") greeting. He followed with a qualitative evaluation ("That was a pretty good dive, but your feet came apart just as you hit the water") and concluded with a suggestion for improvement ("Go up and give it another try and this time keep those toes pointed"). The matter was not closed. The evaluation was personal, gave the coach's general response to the dive, and gave directions on how to continue to develop better diving skills.

> The most fluid form for getting an impression of a person through the eyes of a second person is to invite the second person to talk or write to you about him.[4]

Use Words

This is the same type of response we would expect in a checkup from our personal physicians. But what if you went to your doctor for a physical and at the end of a battery of tests and poking around, she calls you into her office and says, "C+," and walks out? I think you would be pretty upset and probably wouldn't tolerate such a response. Yet most teachers put a number or letter on an assignment or test and return it. Fewer write comments throughout the assignment or test. Even a comment like "well done" is often interpreted by the student as a response to the grade marked rather than the quality of the assignment or assessment.

What we forget is that the grade, score, or percent written at the top has already terminated the exercise. Even though the assignment is still not completed to the quality required, evaluating it with a number or letter has brought the experience to closure. The student gets the message that this is now done and over, finished. In forgiving learning, there are no numbers or letters put on any assignment or assessment results. Verbal and written comments affirm what the student has done well, what has been done poorly, and then what needs to be done to improve the quality to meet the coach's standards.

These ideas are not new. Humans know how to teach humans. It was Francis de La Mothe-Fenclon, in his writings on the education of girls in the seventeenth century, who said,

> Do not speak of a defect to a child without adding some method of overcoming it that many encourage the attempt, for the mortification and discouragement that cold correction produces must be avoided.[5]

Accepting Mediocrity

What has happened thus far in education is that we continue to accept assignments and assessments from students that are less than what demonstrates mastery of the concepts. We tolerate that which does not convince us that the student really does have a grasp of the task at hand. So we satisfy ourselves with less than what is possible and reasonable, just so we can record the assignment with a grade and move on to the next topic.

This is not the way it is in the real world. Even if you work at McDonald's and are putting together an order for a cheeseburger, fries, and a soda, you cannot demand your salary if you do everything correct but leave off the cheese. You cannot go to your supervisor and argue that you got 90 percent of the order correct, which is an A. McDonald's requires 100 percent of the work done. This is why in forgiving learning, when a below-par assignment is submitted, it is returned to be worked on according to the comments written on the paper. It may have to be done many times over until it is completed to the quality requested.

My son, who is a structural engineer, tells me his plans are "redlined" (i.e., marked for corrections) over and over by other engineers until it is done up to specifications. Buildings could fall and people could die if it's just done 90 percent correct.

A PRIVILEGE, NOT A RIGHT

Following each unit of study there is a student-teacher conference. This is the summative experience in which the student has the opportunity to demonstrate his/her mastery of the concepts covered. In order to qualify for this conference, the students must present a portfolio of all their assignments (all of which will have been completed up to the teacher's standards). In forgiving learning, the student-teacher conference then becomes the summative assessment medium. But in the forgiving learning system, this evaluation is not a *right*; it is a *privilege* for those who have done all the unit assignments to the instructor's standards.

IF YOU DON'T PRACTICE, YOU DON'T PLAY

I don't know any coach who doesn't live by this adage. Playing in the game, participating in the match is a privilege and not a right. It is reserved for those who have followed the basic physics' principle: You can only take energy out of a system if you have first put energy into it. Or, in social terms, "You don't get something for nothing." There is merit to the view that being assessed is a privilege for those who have put out the effort and persistence in the learning experience.

It is rewarding for athletes to see how well they can perform outside daily practice sessions. It is rewarding for teenagers to see how well they can drive a car outside the classroom simulator. It can be very satisfying for students to see how their instructor and/or other evaluators respond to their display of what they have learned. Students will value various types of assessments if they can appreciate that they have worked for the opportunity to demonstrate to themselves and others how much they have accomplished.

STUDENT-TEACHER CONFERENCE

How then does a student come to show mastery of each unit? Once again, it is simple: Complete each and every assignment to the instructor's satisfaction to qualify for the student-teacher conference. Then, in the conference with your teacher, prove that you have a grasp of the key elements of the unit. I tell the students that I expect them to demonstrate in some fashion what they know and/or can do.

> "Think of the driving test," said San Luis Obispo High School's English department chair, Ivan Simon. "If you just looked at how well someone answered the written part of the driver's test, then you'd assume the skill of the driver was represented by only that score. But that person wouldn't necessarily be a good driver."[6]

JUSTIFY ANSWERS

There are no hidden agendas or attempts to use "tricky" questions in the student-teacher conference. A key aspect of each question is the requirement that students justify their answers—that is, explain their thinking or provide some evidence of their understanding. This requires thought and reflective defense of their responses. The conference is held in some isolated part of the room. If students respond to my satisfaction that they have demonstrated mastery of that concept, we repeat this process for the remaining two or three questions. If they do not master a question, they have the opportunity to return at another time to attempt a nuanced form of the same question.

They may return as often as they wish at some mutually agreed time, with no penalty, until they have convinced me they understand. In forgiving learning, students' errors are forgiven and they are given other opportunities to demonstrate their understanding. Other options to a student-teacher conference are some type of project or classroom presentation that covers the same concepts. Once again, a weak performance can be repeated at a different time, covering the same learning goals.

FORGIVING LEARNING

I originally experienced this idea from my high school football coach. When I first went out for football I wanted to play middle linebacker. To make a long story short, I wasn't very good. But as the season progressed I got better and better. At the end of the season we were going to play our archrival. I started the game.

My coach played me at first string for the first time. He didn't tell me, "You know, Lucido, at the beginning of the season you were lousy, now you're pretty good, so that means you are average and you can't start." No, he looked for progress and where I was at the end of the season, not somewhere in the past where the "sins" of my failings were. He forgave those and put them behind us.

I'm sure this story doesn't stand alone in coaching annals, but it brings to light a critically important concept—never take hope away from a learner. I don't think any one of us wants to be judged by our past failings, but how those experiences have given rise to a wiser, healthier, and more competent person in the present.

> As long as students feel there is more risk in making errors than there is payoff in learning, they will remain passive learners.[7]

MIRROR LIFE—NOT AVERAGES

During the 2008 Super Bowl, the New York Giants played the New England Patriots. The Giants had a 10–6 regular season record and had lost to the Patriots just a few weeks before. The Patriots were 16–0 and a heavy favorite to win. The Giants won the Super Bowl. What was important is not where either team was during the season, but at the end of the season during the Super Bowl. Life is not about averages but about the present moment. Assessments should mirror life. In forgiving learning, no longer is the "test" over and done with and thrown in the garbage can, purged from students' short-term memory. The opportunity to return again and again until mastery is achieved is the fertile soil for learning.

It is interesting to note that since I have been using this forgiving learning process, I have heard students talk much more about the concepts they have or have not mastered and significantly less about their grades. I have seen students helping each other in talking about these concepts, using everyday examples to illustrate their understanding. I have seen students listen to each other in a way that was extremely rare before.

QUANTUM LEAP

I have wondered if this kind of forgiving learning really has produced a quantum leap from "test-day learning" to long-term learning. For years my intuition would tell me that how a student performed on a test was not nearly as valid as what they had accomplished during the regular part of the course. This sense is supported by the research of Conway, Cohen, and Stanhope in their paper "Why Is it That University Grades Do Not Predict Very-Long-Term Retention?":

> The findings imply that the standard achieved in course work is a more sensitive indicator of knowledge acquisition (and consequent retention) than are examinations. . . . From our studies of cognitive psychology and memory for a work of literature (Conway et al., 1991; Stanhope et al., 1992), it seems clear that examinations are not sensitive to the amount of knowledge acquired. Maybe, as Bahrick (1992) suggested, examination grades are primarily awarded on the basis of knowledge retained in the short term, knowledge that the student rapidly acquired and almost as rapidly lost.[8]

My students' responses to a questionnaire I gave after their final grades were recorded regarding the forgiving learning process seem to anecdotally corroborate these studies. I believe that if my students are telling me that they are experiencing a kind of learning that will last longer than test-day learning, then this is a first step in putting faith in forgiving learning.

What follows is a representative sample of what my students said in response to this prompt:

Should I use the forgiving learning process with student-teacher mastery conferences instead of standard classroom methods using written tests next year? Why or why not? Do you think you will remember what you've learned more using the forgiving learning process with student-teacher mastery conferences than tests? Why or why not?

"With mastery you retain a lot more because you are talking about what you learn."

"I think mastery is better because you have to learn it. On tests people cram the night before then forget everything."

"Definitely!! Do not stop masteries. I have learned so much more this year and I feel like I retain it so much better with masteries. You don't ask us to regurgitate what we've read, but make us apply it to other situations."

"On a written test we still don't remember everything we did afterwards. Mastery makes us learn more because we have to know how something works as well as why and be ready for anything."

"For the written tests I can cram and then forget, but I remember more from mastery conferences."

"This way you can decide whether we know the concepts and we can't B.S."

"You get a chance for those who are slow learners to understand the concept."

"Tests are too impersonal and once we've studied for them and take them we forget them. With mastery on a more personal, one on one basis, allows for better relationship thus allowing, me anyway, to remember the material and I have learned."

"Mastery conferences are a challenge but you are able to try again which makes it good. I think you will remember more because you are more pressured to learn. If you take a test you could easily copy."

"When you have mastery there is not a feeling of fear because you can come back. Plus, in a test, if you get it wrong . . . whoopee! You get it wrong and forget about it. In mastery you are forced to learn."

"I learned more by mastery, it makes me think more and understand better, it's a definite yes. I remember much more with mastery than test. It also improves my ability to speak with others better. It builds my confidence."

"When you take tests it is just memorizing answers. Mastery is more personal and you have to remember the concepts you have learned, not just memorize them and forget them later."

"In my particular case, when the word test or quiz or anything of the sort is mentioned something in my brain says, 'forget everything you know!' I tend to worry a lot about my grades and the thought of messing up or in a sense failing scares me a bit. One good thing that I appreciate in this grading system is the fact that you have the option to come back for mastery as many times as needed and that in a sense I would think it also shows you how dedicated some people are to mastering a unit."

"Mastery conferences are an advantage for me because I have time to understand what was taught in that certain unit. It also gives me an idea about how much I really understand. It also helps me with one of my problems; the problem of not being able to explain things to others."

"Although I am an A student I have grasped all the concepts in physics more so than in any other science class."

"Simply put, the method that is used to teach this class is, by far, the best that I have encountered in my eleven years of attending school. . . . I honestly believe that the logs have been of utmost importance in increasing the rate of comprehension. . . . I wouldn't revise any part of the system, for I know that I will retain what I have learned longer that anything else I have ever 'mastered.'"

"The part I like the most about how you teach are the mastery conferences. Because it's not a multiple guess or other written exams where we throw our minds to the paper to pass, it's you who we have to convince we've passed. This makes us study harder and more thoroughly since we don't have an idea of what you are going to ask us. Also, just the thought of an oral exam makes us nervous and so it encourages us to make every effort to answer correctly and support our answers to the best of our ability rather than just remembering the answers and writing them down on a piece of paper. We actually have to think!"

"Because then you must be prepared for everything."

"I think you should keep mastery conferences because this way I learn 100%. But in a regular situation I could learn only 90% of the material and still get an A."

This anecdotal qualitative "data" and the experiences of the last twenty-five years of my teaching have convinced me that I am onto something here.

STUDENTS COME FIRST

Learning makes sense to students when we stop marching from topic to topic and chapter to chapter while quizzing and testing along the way with little regard for the student's true level of comprehension. A coach wouldn't think about introducing an advanced play to the football team unless it can run simpler plays effectively. Let's not doggedly follow the course outline with more concern for the district and/or state high-stakes testing than with the healthy progress of the children in our charge. We teach students. We do not teach courses or subjects or grade levels. If we can't tell the difference between the prior two sentences, therein lies a major problem.

Concern for students should come before concern for the topic. Academic coaching means changing our teaching attitude from classroom manager to professional mentor and facilitator. It means using all our creativity to teach in a relevant manner. It means creating a team spirit within our classrooms with cooperation winning out over coercion.

It means seeing each student as a person who really wants to know, but who probably has been preconditioned to believe otherwise. It means placing a higher value on forgiveness and hope than on justice and punishment. It means using the forgiving learning process to enable students to overcome the fear of their teacher, the fear of fellow students, the fear of the course content, and the fear of their grades.

> Better courses, better curriculum, better coverage, better teaching machines will never resolve our dilemma in a basic way. Only persons acting like persons in their relationships with the students can even begin to make a dent on this most urgent problem of modern education.[9]

ABOLISH HIGH-STAKES TESTS

The greatest walls that confine the true artistic work of teachers are high-stakes tests, grades, and scores. They are the tip of the shark's fin. They are what we see; they are the day-to-day practical extension of the corporate supported, competitive high-stakes testing system. We have presented rational and effective reasons to support its elimination. As high-stakes tests are abolished, one of the results will be that we will quickly see revealed some of the attitudes that have lain hidden beneath the surface.

> The grading system vitally determines what the teacher will include in his class, what he will omit, and what he will require of students so he can justify the "grade" he must give. The kinds of tests given and how they are graded are often thus determined. Often, the entire system has the effect of so occupying teachers with the necessities of that system, that we often do not permit ourselves to really look at the side effects or consequences of that system.[10]

The forgiving learning process I offer is a brain-compatible solution. Coaches' evaluative interactions with their athletes involve times of encouragement and praise, times of constructive criticism, and times of direction for improvement. This is not accomplished by good wishes but by intentional classroom design. In summary, the central hallmarks of the forgiving learning process include the following:

- The teacher must take on the mindset of a coach. Enthusiasm for students and topics studied is a key element.
- The learning experience must be designed to maximize student comprehension, not to prepare for external high-stakes testing.
- Content is to be made relevant and meaningful to students.
- Praise, constructive criticism, and suggestions for improvement must constitute the basis for every response to a student's work and assessment.
- Written and/or oral comments must replace scores and grades on all student work.
- Mistakes are a part of the learning process. Accepting errors without punishment must become a common practice in all that students do.
- Requiring that 100 percent of assignments be done with unlimited resubmissions until quality has been achieved is a real-life goal.
- Some form of student-teacher mastery conferences, demonstrations, presentations, and the like, which provide multiple sources of evidence of what students know and are able to do, is both a valid and a satisfying experience for students and teachers.
- The ability to revisit weaknesses discovered during the mastery conference gives the student the sense that forgiveness is real and progress is more important than grades and scores.
- Forgiving learning must be used as a key component of any grading process, which includes a meeting with students and their self-evaluation.
- Teaming reduces anxiety by changing the relationship with fellow students from that of competitors to a cooperative sense of camaraderie.

To me the worst thing seems to be for a school principally to work with methods of fear, force, and artificial authority. Such treatment destroys the sound sentiments, the sincerity, and the self-confidence of the pupil. It produces the submissive subject. . . . It is comparatively simple to keep the school free from this worst of all evils. Give into the power of the teacher the fewest possible coercive measures, so that the only source of the pupil's respect for the teacher is the human and intellectual qualities of the latter.[11] (Albert Einstein)

CONCLUSION

Unlike electrons or billiard balls, students have ambitions and purposes and refuse to be treated as lumps of clay or sheets of steel passively awaiting the impact of a scientifically based teaching technology that provides little or no scope in its assumptions for what students make of all of this . . . and even when we succeed in shaping our students surfaces, unless we touch their souls we will be locked out of their inner lives.[12]

What Professor Elliot Eisner has said in the quote above is at the core of my work. Students as people are the beginning and end of the educational endeavor. They are free persons by nature and by the declaration of our country's Constitution. Our compulsory education laws are not just compulsory in requiring the student to attend school but just as compulsory in requiring us to attend to them.

How can we expect students to be eager to learn unless they are having concrete experiences of their teachers, school, and district as advocates for their personal educational welfare? Few of us want to be in places where we are distrusted, regimented, and frightened. High-stakes testing, preparation, and the resulting excessive focus on scores are the signs of the times that tell us we've gone too far. We are killing our children's desire to learn and substituting false, superficial goals. This testing mania cuts across all student ages, grade levels, cultures, languages, and sexes.

It truly is an educational genocide of untold proportions. It is a silent killer, a plague on our children that will make itself known in a shallow-thinking, self-serving society based on acquisition and blind obedience to corporate directives. My dad worked at a steel plant for forty-two years, where he tested sheets of metal, measured and recorded their various ranges of hardness, and scored them for use by the customer. But students are people, human beings who are not like sheets of metal. They are subjects and not objects.

They seek out human interaction whenever possible. They want to learn and not be measured at every turn. Teachers know how to be sensitive coaches, mentors, and masters of our art of instructing students. Teachers are the professional extension of a child's parents while in their charge. They need the autonomy and support to do it.

If society continues believing students don't want to learn, teachers don't want to teach, and administrators don't want to administer, we will sustain and nurture the hierarchy of fear and distrust that supports the oppression and anxiety that high-stakes testing produces. All too soon, they have become the rigid walls that separate us from our students, and our students from what learning is all about. They anesthetize our senses to the reality of our students' lives.

This testing system does not want us to take individual student cases into consideration, because the high-stakes testing mindset is based on the false assumption that all students are alike and must be tested, graded, and scored without any partiality. Even our remedial prescriptions often utilize the rigid language of inflexibility—the fallout of our quantification processes:

> How could anyone smugly prescribe "intellectual rigor" for Sherryl, whose parents had just separated, leaving her bewildered and half-crippled by anxiety? What did "concentration on subject matter content" mean to Harold, who sometimes came to school tired and hungry?[13]

The corporate-industrial model of education, while pretending to be scientific, does not want teachers to be flexible for one student, because then we will have locked ourselves into the logic that we'd have the apparently impossible task of being flexible for everyone. Assembly-line thinking is based on sameness, not exception. It creates an atmosphere of fear for those educators and students who "step out of line" by not following their assigned roles in the education machine. Flexibility, sensitivity, and exceptions cannot be quantified and so cannot become part of the system. There is no place in the production line for teachers to be understanding.

This pressures teachers into thinking they are being "just" when they give in to the high-stakes test, grade, and score mentality. The system requires us to quantify and normalize instead of qualify and personalize. It's a lot easier to think and behave as if one is being objective and impersonal. To admit that one is a human dealing with other humans makes schooling a more intimate experience than the corporate-industrial model allows.

> The dissolution of freedom in the torturous crushing of real public school reform is by people who haven't the slightest idea of what it means to teach in a world of all kinds of kids with all kinds of minds with all kinds of learning styles from all kinds of backgrounds from all kinds of socioeconomic and family conditions with all kinds of wants and needs.[14]

Throughout history, revolutions in many lands laid bare the injustices and improprieties in the operation of the ruling governments. This work, in unison with the many other works of educators, parents, students, and concerned citizens, attempts to reveal the glaring deficiencies of our school system and constructive options for change. There is much precedent for the transformation of many unjust and unproductive societies. This gives us hope that the suggestions presented here are possible and that change is not outside our power.

Our industrial model of schooling has been with us for over one hundred years. It has really only been in the last thirty or so years that the intensity of focus has been to attempt to employ corporate policies and practices that pretend to be scientific with our usage of and preparation for high-stakes testing, grades, and scores. We as educators, parents, students, and concerned citizens can alter our direction.

I, like many of you, am sick and tired of hearing "We can't change the system—it's too big!" If a ragtag army could defeat a system of British colonial rule, we too can again become masters of our schools and not its slaves and lackeys. A revolution in the system can only come about with a change in the hearts and minds of all involved.

> Never doubt that a small group of thoughtful committed citizens can change the world. Indeed, it is the only thing that ever has. (Margaret Mead)

The impetus for this openness to change does not come from analyzing declining test scores, production line output, or the gross national product. It comes about from looking into the eyes of a child and there seeing all you long to be and all that they can be. What excites me most is to imagine high school students just as eager to walk into my classroom as my children were to go to kindergarten each day. I long to see what Edgar Z. Freedenberg[15] so perceptibly envisioned: "Then, there may come a time when you can't even tell education from living." There is something for each of us to do tomorrow.

Notes

CHAPTER 1

1. Stephen Jay Gould. (1981). *The Mismeasure of Man* (Norton, New York), 24.

2. Robert Glasser, Lamar Alexander, and H. Thomas James. (1987). "The Nation's Report Card: Improving the Assessment of Student Achievement," The National Academy of Education.

3. Gould (1981), 24.

4. W. James Popham. (2001). *The Truth about Testing* (ASCD, Alexandria, VA).

5. Bronwyn T. Williams. (2005). "Standardized Students: The Problems with Writing for Tests Instead of People," *Journal of Adolescent & Adult Literacy*, Vol. 49, No. 2 (October), 152–58.

6. Mike Ditka. (2006). Comment during a Cardinals vs. Bears Telecast, August 25.

7. Carlos Garcia, superintendent of Fresno Unified School District. (1999). "Vision for Success," presentation at a district-wide meeting, January 14.

8. Isaiah Berlin. (1996). "On Political Judgment," *The New York Review of Books*, October 3.

9. Marilyn Cochran-Smith. (2006). "Taking Stock in 2006, Evidence, Evidence Everywhere," *Journal of Teacher Education*, Vol. 57, No. 1, (January/February), 6.

10. Alfie Kohn. (2000). *The Case against Standardized Testing* (Heinemann, Portsmouth, NH), 3.

11. George E. Hein, professor emeritus, Lesley University. (2007). "Bias in Tests," posting to ndsgroup@yahoogroups.com, February 2.

12. Anthony Cody. (2008). "Rising Scores May Not Mean Students Are Learning More," *San Jose Mercury News*, Opinion Column, May 1.

13. Michael Winerip. (2005). "Are Schools Passing or Failing? Now There's a Third Choice . . . Both," *New York Times*, November 2.

14. Annette Dunlap. (2005). "Standardized Testing Dumbs Down Education— Today's Over-Tested Students Lack the Genuine Spirit of Inquiry," *Charlotte Observer*, October 27.

CHAPTER 2

1. Richard P. Sloan. (2006). "The Critical Distinction between Science and Religion," in *Blind Faith: The Unholy Alliance of Religion and Medicine* (St. Martin's Press, New York).

2. Charles Murray. (2006). "Acid Tests: No Child Left Behind Is Uninformative. It Is Deceptive," *Wall Street Journal*, July 25.

3. Ken Goodman. (2008). "The Pulse: Education's Place for Debate," February 5.

4. Meteor Blades. (2007). "Jim Cummins Demolishes NCLB's Ideology and Practice," *Daily Kos*, July 26, www.dailykos.com/storyonly/2007/7/26/131722/394.

5. Stephen Jay Gould. (1981). *The Mismeasure of Man* (Norton, New York), 21–27, 78.

6. American Evaluation Association Board of Directors. (2002). "Violations of AEA Guiding Principles and Other Professional Standards," February.

7. Gould (1981).

8. Bruce Bower. (1997). "Null Science," *Science News*, June 7.

9. S. Messick. (1989). *Educational Measurement*, third ed. (Macmillan, New York), 14ff.

10. Alfie Kohn. (2000). *The Case against Standardized Testing* (Heinemann, Portsmouth, NH).

11. Knowledge Networks. (2008). AP Poll, Menlo Park, CA, interview dates: June 18 and 23, 2008.

12. "Making Teens Start School in the Morning is 'Cruel,' Brain Doctor Claims." (2008). *London Evening Standard*, June 10, www.thisislondon.co.uk/news/article-23381421-details/Making+teens+start+school+in+the+morning+is+'cruel',+brain+doctor+claims/article.do.

13. Lisa Heschong, project director, California Energy Commission. (2003). "Windows and Classrooms: A Study of Student Performance and the Indoor Environment," P500-03-082-A-7 Heschong Mahone Group, Inc., Fair Oaks, California, September.

14. Emily Hobson/CalJustice. (2003). "First Things First," May 17, 10, www.caljustice.org/cfj_live/images/stories/2003_First_Things_First.pdf .

15. Bronwyn T. Williams. (2005). "Standardized Students: The Problems with Writing for Tests Instead of People," *Journal of Adolescent & Adult Literacy*, Vol. 49, No. 2 (October), 152–58.

CHAPTER 3

1. W. James Popham. (2001). *The Truth about Testing* (ASCD, Alexandria, VA), 16, 25, 75.

2. Peter Henry. (2007). "The Case against Standardized Testing," *Minnesota English Journal*, December.

3. Elizabeth Schultz. (1992). "Enemy of Innovation—Our Obsession with Standardized Testing Is Impeding Reform," *Teacher Magazine*, September 29.

4. Rick Stiggins. (2007). "Educational Testing Service's Assessment Training Institute," *Ed Week*, Vol. 27, Issue 8 (October 17), 28–29.

5. Peter Magnuson. (2000). "High-Stakes Cheating: Will the Focus on Accountability Lead to More Cheating?" *Communicator* (February), 1, 3.

6. National Commission for the Protection of Human Subjects of Biomedical and Behavioral Research. (1974). National Research Act of 1974, Public Law 93-348, July.

7. David Glovin and David Evans. (2006). "How Test Companies Fail Your Kids," *Bloomberg Markets*, December 1.

8. Popham (2001).

9. Michael Beadle. (2008). *Smokey Mountain News*, May 21.

10. Juanita Doyon. (2008). "Seattle Teacher Refuses to Administer WASL Test to Students, Citing Multiple Harms Test Causes Students, Teachers, Schools, and Parents," Parent Empowerment Network, Spanaway, Washington, April 20, www .parentempowermentnetwork.org.

11. Juan Gonzalez. (2008). "Bronx 8th-Graders Boycott Practice Exam but Teacher May Get Ax," *New York Daily News*, May 22.

12. Regina Brett. (2008). "Students Pass State Test, But at What Cost to Their Education?" *Cleveland Plain Dealer*, July 22.

13. Valerie Strauss. (2006). "The Rise of the Testing Culture: As Exam-Takers Get Younger, Some Say Value Is Overblown," *Washington Post*, October 10.

CHAPTER 4

1. Dennis M. D. Gersten. (1998). "The Modern Oath of Hippocrates," www .imagerynet.com/hippo.ama.html.

2. Linda Darling-Hammond. (2009). "What Is Genuine Accountability?" California Professional Development Consortia, Asilomar, November.

3. California Commission on Teacher Credentialing and California Department of Education. (1997). California Standards for the Teaching Profession, January.

4. Western Association of Schools and Colleges Accrediting Commission for Schools. (2009). "Why WASC?" www.acswasc.org/about_why.htm.

5. Fredrick M. Hess. (2003). "The Case for Being Mean," American Enterprise Institute, December 1, www.frederickhess.org/5049/the-case-for-being-mean.

6. Don McIntosh. (2005). "Schools' 'Broad' Agenda," *Willamette Week Online*, May 5, www.wweek.com/editorial/3226/7507.

7. L. M. McNeil, E. Coppola, J. Radigan, and J. Vasquez Heilig. (2008). "Avoidable Losses: High-Stakes Accountability and the Dropout Crisis," *Education Policy Analysis Archives* (January).

8. Claudia Wallis. (2008). "No Child Left Behind—Doomed to Fail," *Time Magazine*, June 8.

9. Monty Neil. (2008). "McClellan Tell-All Exposes Media's Propaganda Problem," June 14, arn-l@interversity.org.

CHAPTER 5

1. Mary Compton and Lois Weiner, eds. (2008). *The Global Assault on Teachers, Teaching and Teacher Unions* (Palgrave Macmillan, New York), 4.

2. Barbara Miner. (2002). "For-Profits Target Education," *Rethinking Schools* (Spring), 2.

3. Fredrick M. Hess, ed. (2006). *Educational Entrepreneurship: Realities, Challenges, Possibilities* (Harvard Education Press, Cambridge, MA), 252.

4. Campbell, Peter. (2006). Transform Education Blog, posted January 21, http://transformeducation.blogspot.com/2006/01/competition-and-education.html.

5. National Commission on Excellence in Education. (1983). *A Nation at Risk* (U.S. Government Printing Office, Washington, DC).

6. Patricia French. (2002). "Quality—If Its Not Measurable, Does It Matter?" School of Management Conference Paper, The Open Polytechnic of New Zealand.

7. Kathy Emery. (2005). Part of a panel presentation at the San Francisco State University faculty retreat, Asilomar, California, January 26, www.educationanddemocracy.org/Emery/Emery_NCLB.htm.

8. Alain Jehlen. (2007). "Testing: How the Sausage Is Made . . . What's in a Score?" *NEA Today* (January), www.nea.org/neatoday/0701/score.html.

9. Iris C. Rotberg. (2008). "Quick Fixes, Test Scores, and the Global Economy—Myths That Continue to Confound Us," *Ed Week*, Vol. 27, Issue 41 (June 11), 27, 32.

10. Gerald Bracey. (2008). "A letter to Jonathan Alter of *Newsweek*," July 7, *Huffington Post*, www.huffingtonpost.com.

11. Cindy Long. (2007). "Can We Compete? In the Face of New Global Rivalries, the Answer Is Still Yes—And American Math and Science Education Has the World Watching," *NEA Today* (January).

12. Vivek Wadhwa. (2007). "The Science Education Myth: Forget the Conventional Wisdom," *Business Week*, October 26, www.businessweek.com/smallbiz/content/oct2007/sb20071025_827398.htm; Lindsay Lowell and Harold

Salzman. (2007). "Assessing the Evidence on Science and Engineering Education, Quality, and Workforce Demand," October, www.urban.org/publications/411562 .html.

13. World Economic Forum. (2007/2008). "Global Competitiveness Report Country Profile Highlights," www.weforum.org/en/initiatives/gcp/Global%20Comp etitiveness%20Report/Highlights2008/index.htm.

14. William J. Mathis. (2008). "The Clarity of a Mother's Voice," *Rutland Herald*, January 17.

15. Rick Ayers. (2007). "Testing and Competition." *Huffington Post*, June 28, www. huffingtonpost.com/rick-ayers-/testing-and-competition_b_54216.html.

16. Steve Strauss. (2006). "Teachers Stand Up against Cookie-Cutter Education," *Freedom Socialist*, Vol. 27, No. 5 (October–November).

17. Scott W. Baker. (2006). Letters to the editor, *Muskegon Chronicle*, October 1.

18. Dave Posner. (2001). "Bubble Students and Teaching to the Statistic," *San Jose Mercury News*, March 23.

19. Lawrence A. Cremin. (1990). *Popular Education and Its Discontents* (Harper & Row, New York).

20. Leslie Poyner and Paula M. Wolfe. (2004). *Marketing Fear in America's Public Schools* (Lawrence Erlbaum Associates, Mahwah, NJ), 5.

21. Edward Deci. (1995). *Why We Do What We Do: The Dynamics of Personal Autonomy* (Putnam, New York).

22. Philip Kovacs. (2006). "Gates, Buffett, and the Corporatization of Children," *Common Dreams*, June 28, www.commondreams.org/views06/0628-30.htm.

CHAPTER 6

1. Paulo Freire. (1970). *Pedagogy of the Oppressed* (Continuum, New York).

2. Meris Stansbury. (2008). "U.S. Educators Seek Lessons from Scandinavia High Scoring Nations on an International Exam Say Success Stems from Autonomy, Project-Based Learning," *eSchool News*, March 3, www.eschoolnews.com/news/top-news/?i=52770.

3. William Cala. (2008). "High-Stakes Tests Push Kids to Streets," *Rochester Democrat and Chronicle*, July 27.

4. Nancy Ginsburg Gill. (2007). "Goodbye, Mr. & Ms. Chips," *Education Week*, July 18.

5. California Commission on Teacher Credentialing. (1997). California Standards for the Teaching Profession, adopted January.

6. Anonymous teacher, Florida. (2005). "Overnight, A Bad Teacher?" February 19, www.susanohanian.org/outrage_fetch.php?id=294.

7. Jim Horn. (2007). "What IS left behind?" September 28, www.SchoolsMatter .blogspot.com.

8. William Bonville, secretary of the American Party of Oregon. (2002). Fax (503) 476-5533, or send e-mail to bonville@cdsnet.net, www.cdsnet.net/people/local/ bonville/public_html/obe/obeintro.htm.

9. Gerald Bracey. (2007). "The Inmates Who Want to Run the Asylum," *Huffington Post*, December 12, www.huffingtonpost.com/gerald-bracey/the-inmates-who-want-to-r_b_76560.html.

10. Irv Besecker. (2000). "The Insanity of Testing Mania," *Greensboro N. Carolina News & Record*, June 11.

11. Edward Humes. (2007). "'No Child Left Behind' Should Really Be Called 'No Test Left Behind,'" review of *Tested: One American School Struggles to Make the Grade*, by Linda Perlstein, *Los Angeles Times Book Review*, July 9.

12. Eric Carpenter. (2008). "Teaching Dispute Leads to Parent Picketing and Student Walkout," *The Orange County Register*, January 2.

13. Peter Henry. (2007). "The Case against Standardized Testing," *Minnesota English Journal*, December 12.

CHAPTER 7

1. Jean-Pierre Prevost. (2008). "What Is All This Murmuring About?" *God's Word Today* (June), 46.

2. O. Felix Ayadi, Amitava Chatterjee, and Mammo Woldie. (2006). "Matching Testing Strategy with Student Personality in a Historically Black University," *Journal of College Teaching & Learning*, Vol. 3, No. 3 (March).

3. Fahimeh Marefat. (2006). "Student Writing, Personality Type of the Student and Rater: Any Interrelationship?" *The Reading Matrix*, Vol. 6, No. 2 (September).

4. Gordon Lawrence. (1979). *People Types & Tiger Stripes* (Center for Application of Psychological Type, Gainesville, FL), 42; for data, see Isabel Briggs-Myers and Mary McCauley (1989), *A Guide to the Development and Use of the MBTI Indicator* (Consulting Psychologists Press, Gainesville, FL), 95–139.

5. Linda K. Pratt. (1981). "The Relationship of the Myers-Briggs Type Indicator to Scores on the National Teacher's Examination," AIR Forum Paper.

6. Timothy Chang and Daphne Chang. (2000). *The Role of Myers-Briggs Type Indicator in Electrical Engineering Education, ICEE/Proceedings/papers.*

7. Briggs-Myers and McCauley (1989).

8. Standardized Testing and Reporting (STAR) Program. (2009). "Explaining 2008 STAR Program Student Reports to Parents and Guardians," November 10, www .cde.ca.gov/ta/tg/sr/documents/explnrpts08.pdf.

9. Michael H. Kean. (2004). "No Single Test Does Everything—The Importance of Multiple Measures," CTB/McGraw-Hill, www.maths456.net/wbja/html/48860 .html.

10. California Department of Education and the American Educational Research Association, American Psychological Association, and National Council on Measurement in Education. (2003/2004). *California Department of Education STAR Post-Test Guide Version 1-2004, Standards for Educational and Psychological Testing.*

11. Dave Posner. (2001). "Bubble Students and Teaching to the Statistic," *San Jose Mercury News*, March 23.

12. Kim Hannan. (2008). Teacher e-mail to Rog Lucido, February 29.

13. Alliance for Childhood. (2001). "High-Stakes Testing: A Statement of Concern and Call to Action," position statement, April 25.

14. Associated Press. (2006). "The Admissions Game," Cambridge, MA, September 18, www.mitadmissions.org/topics/before/helping_your_parents_through_this _process/marilee_jones_in_the_news_1.shtml.

15. Jacob Miller. (2007). "MCAS Hinders Student Learning," letter to the editor, *South Coast Today*, October 9.

CHAPTER 8

1. Bernard Gassaway. (2005). "Reflections of an Urban High School Principal," *Education News*, December 12.

2. Richard Rothstein. (2007). "Leaving NCLB Behind," *American Prospect*, December 17, www.prospect.org/cs/articles?article=leaving_nclb_behind.

3. W. Edwards Deming. (1982, 1986). *Out of the Crisis* (MIT Press, Cambridge, MA).

4. Anthony Cody. (2007). "State Schools on Collision Course with Standards," *Fresno Bee*, December 14, B7.

5. National Commission on Excellence in Education. (1983). *A Nation at Risk* (U.S. Government Printing Office, Washington, DC).

6. Christopher H. Tienken. (2008). "Rankings of International Achievement, Test Performance, and Economic Strength: Correlation or Conjecture?" *International Journal of Education Policy & Leadership*, Vol. 3, No. 4 (April 25).

7. Gerald Bracey. (2007). "The Inmates Who Want to Run the Asylum," *Huffington Post*, December 12, www.huffingtonpost.com/gerald-bracey/the-inmates-who-want-to-r_b_76560.html.

8. Frederick M. Hess. (2003). "The Case for Being Mean," American Enterprise Institute, December 1, www.aei.org/issue/19614.

9. Steve Strauss. (2006). "Teachers Stand Up against Cookie-Cutter Education," *Freedom Socialist*, Vol. 27, No. 5 (October–November).

10. Larry Kuehn. (1997). "Schools for Globalized Business: The APEC Agenda for Education," a commentary on the "Concept Paper" for the APEC Human Resources Ministerial Meeting, Corpwatch, British Columbia Teachers' Federation, May 1.

11. Peter Henry. (2007). "The Case against Standardized Testing," *Minnesota English Journal*, December 12.

12. Paulo Freire. (1970). *Pedagogy of the Oppressed* (Continuum Publishing, New York), 60.

CHAPTER 9

1. Beth Boyer. (2007). "How Sad I Feel (or I Hate NCLB)," e-mail to Rog Lucido, September 14.

2. California Commission on Teacher Credentialing, California Department of Education. (1997). "California Standards for the Teaching Profession," January.

3. Esperanza Renteria. (2002). "Teaching to Change LA: An Educational Bill of Rights," *Online Journal for IDEA*, Issue No. 3, Vol. 2, No. 1–10 (March 11), www .tcla.gseis.ucla.edu/rights/features/3/student/acosta3.html.

4. Chris Sloan. (2008). "Students Are People, Not Numbers: What Will It Take to Get Teachers to Refuse to Participate in a System That Harms Children?" *The San Angelo Standard-Times*, March 4.

5. Alliance for Childhood. (2001). "High-Stakes Testing: A Statement of Concern and Call to Action," position statement, April 25.

6. Nancy Ginsburg Gill. (2007). "Goodbye, Mr. & Ms. Chips," *Education Week*, July 18.

7. Juliet Williams. (2008). "School Districts Face Sanctions," Associated Press, January 15.

8. Janet Steffenhagen. (2007). "Teacher in Hot Water Over Not Giving Test— Colleagues Plan to Rally in Support of Educator," *Vancouver Sun*, September 25.

9. Susan Ohanian. (2007). "Weep for Our Profession: The Corporate Politicos Are Killing It, Scene: Wake County Schools," North Carolina teacher's e-mail, September 12.

10. Marilyn Desbrow. (2007). "Too Much Pressure," *Pasadena Star News*, November 25.

11. Eric Carpenter. (2008). "Teaching Dispute Leads to Parent Picketing and Student Walkout," *The Orange County Register*, January 2.

12. Dave Zweifel. (2007). "Teacher Shows Folly of No Child," *The Capital Times*, November 7.

13. Anne E. Levin Garrison. (2006). "A Second Letter from a Parent," December 7, www.susanohanian.org/show_nclb_atrocities.html?id=2478.

14. Tabitha Cardenas. (2008). "One Mother's Story about Test Intimidation" e-mail, March 21, www.susanohanian.org/search_letters.php.

15. Jack O'Connell. (2004). "Schools Chief Jack O'Connell Announces Proposed Changes to California's NCLB Accountability Workbook," News Release: #04-18, February 25.

16. Catherine Ross Hamel and Fred L. Hamel. (2003). "State-Mandated Testing: Why We Opt Out," *Education Week*, March 12.

17. Paul Shaker. (2008). "Business, Conscience, and Teaching," *Ed Week*, January 9.

18. Staff. (1998). "Teacher Defies Test Rule," *New York Times*, July 15.

19. Percy Ednalino. (2001). "Teacher Won't Administer CSAP Tests," *Denver Post*, January 27.

20. Staff. (2008). "Individual Acts of Resistance," *FairTest Examiner*, July 11.

21. Ralph Blumenthal. (2005). "A School Exam's Conscientious Objector," *New York Times*, February 24.

CHAPTER 10

1. Susan Ohanian. (2008). *When Childhood Collides with NCLB*, Vermont Society for the Study of Education, Inc.

2. Greta Schulz. (2008). "Economic Uncertainty or Excuse-Making?" *St. Louis Business Journal*, February 29, http://atlanta.bizjournals.com/stlouis/stories/2008/03/03/smallb2.html?page=2.

3. John E. Adams. (2008). "Start an Internet Business: How to Make a Start in Business without Making Excuses," March 11, www.content4reprint.com/business/start-an-internet-business-how-to-make-a-start-in-business-without-making-excuses.htm.

4. Ron Edmonds. (1973). Kentucky Department of Education web page, www.education.ky.gov/KDE/Instructional+Resources/Closing+the+Gap/.

5. Rowland Unified School District. (2009). "No Excuses University," www.rowlandschools.org/apps/news/show_news.jsp?REC_ID=110742&id=0.

6. Public School Insights. (2008). "Greenway Elementary: Empowering Educators to Close the Achievement Gap," www.publicschoolinsights.org/greenway-elementary-empowering-educators-close-achievement-gap.

7. George W. Bush. (2001). Remarks by the president in Small Business Roundtable, Control Concepts, Pittsburgh, Pennsylvania, February 28, www.whitehouse.gov/news/releases/2001/02/20010228-10.html.

8. Richard Rothstein. (2008). "Whose Problem Is Poverty?" *Educational Leadership*, Vol. 65, No. 7 (April).

9. Michael Jordan. "Great Sayings," http://greatsayings.blogspot.com/2006/06/michael-jordan-quotes.html (accessed April 7, 2010).

10. Smithsonian staff. (1988). *Inventors*, Smithsonian, July 19.

11. William Cala, a professor at Nazareth College and former interim superintendent, City School District. (2008). "High-Stakes Tests Push Kids to Streets," *Rochester Democrat and Chronicle*, July 27.

12. Glenda Puett. (2008). "A Teacher's Note," April 15, www.susanohanian.org/show_atrocities.html?id=7959.

CHAPTER 11

1. American Association for the Advancement of Science. (1989). *Project 2061 Science for all Americans*, 148.

2. Canadian Health Network. (2004). "School Anxiety? What You Can Do to Help Your Child," August 23, www.medicalnewstoday.com/articles/12414.php.

3. Carl R. Rogers. (1969). *Freedom to Learn* (Charles Merrill, Columbus, OH), 125.

4. Robert L. Thorndike and Elizabeth Hogan. (1961). *Measurement and Evaluation in Psychology and Education* (John Wiley, New York), 351.

5. John S. Brubacken. (1966). *A History of the Problems of Education* (McGraw-Hill, New York), 192.

6. Bryan Dickerson. (2005). "This Is Only a Test: Are the Stakes Too High for a Flawed System?" *New Times San Luis Obisbo*, August 11, www.newtimesslo.com/index.php?p=showarticle&id=1248.

7. Thomas L. Good. (1981). "Teacher Expectations and Student Perceptions: A Decade of Research," *Educational Leadership* (February), 415–21.

8. Martin A. Conway, Gillian Cohen, and Nicola Stanhope. (1992). "Why Is It That University Grades Do Not Predict Very-Long-Term Retention?" *Journal of Experimental Psychology: General*, Vol. 121, No. 3, 383–84.

9. Rogers (1969), 125.

10. Marshal Fisher. (1976). "What's In A Grade," *CSTA Journal* (February), 6.

11. Albert Einstein. (1981). *Ideas and Opinions* (Dell, New York), 69.

12. Elliot W. Eisner. (1983). "The Art and Craft of Teaching," *Educational Leadership* (January), 9.

13. George B. Leonard. (1968). *Education and Ecstasy* (Delacorte Press, New York), 136.

14. Peter Majoy. (2005). Thread III: "NCLB's Ideological Underpinning," Assessment Reform Network List posting, August 27.

15. Beatrice Gross and Ronald Gross. (1970). *Radical School Reform* (Simon & Schuster, New York), 147.

Bibliography

Adams, John E. "Start an Internet Business: How to Make a Start in Business without Making Excuses." March 11, 2008, www.content4reprint.com/business/start-an-internet-business-how-to-make-a-start-in-business-without-making-excuses.htm.

Alliance for Childhood. "High-Stakes Testing: A Statement of Concern and Call to Action" (position statement), April 25, 2001.

American Association for the Advancement of Science. *Project 2061 Science for All Americans*, 1989.

American Evaluation Association Board of Directors. "Violations of AEA Guiding Principles and Other Professional Standards." February 2002.

Anonymous teacher, Florida. "Overnight, a Bad Teacher?" www.susanohanian.org/outrage_fetch.php?id=294, February 19, 2005.

Associated Press. "The Admissions Game," Cambridge, MA, www.mitadmissions.org/topics/before/helping_your_parents_through_this_process/marilee_jones_in_the_news_1.shtml (accessed September 19, 2006).

Ayadi, O. Felix, Amitava Chatterjee, and Mammo Woldie. "Matching Testing Strategy with Student Personality in a Historically Black University." *Journal of College Teaching & Learning*, Vol. 3, No. 3, (March 2006).

Ayers, Rick. "Testing and Competition." *Huffington Post.* www.huffingtonpost.com/rick-ayers-/testing-and-competition_b_54216.html (accessed June 28, 2007).

Baker, Scott W. "Letters to the Editor." *Muskegon Chronicle*, October 1, 2006.

Beadle, Michael. *Smokey Mountain News*, May 21, 2008.

Benziger, Katherine. *The Art Of Using Your Whole Brain.* Dillon, CO: KBA Publications, 1989, 2000.

Besecker, Irv. "The Insanity of Testing Mania." *Greensboro N. Carolina News & Record*, June 11, 2000.

Berlin, Isaiah. "On Political Judgment." *The New York Review of Books*, October 3, 1996.

Blades, Meteor. "Jim Cummins Demolishes NCLB's Ideology and Practice." *Daily Kos*, www.dailykos.com/storyonly/2007/7/26/131722/394 (accessed July 26, 2007).

Blumenthal, Ralph. "A School Exam's Conscientious Objector." *New York Times*, February 24, 2005.

Bonville, William. Secretary of the American Party of Oregon, fax (503) 476-5533, or send e-mail to bonville@cdsnet.net. Website: www.cdsnet.net/people/local/bonville/public_html/obe/obeintro.htm (accessed 2002).

Bower, Bruce. "Null Science." *Science News*, June 7, 1997.

Boyer, Beth. "How Sad I Feel (or I Hate NCLB)." E-mail sent to Rog Lucido, September 14, 2007.

Bracey, Gerald. "The Inmates Who Want to Run the Asylum." *The Huffington Post*, www.huffingtonpost.com/gerald-bracey/the-inmates-who-want-to-r_b_76560.html (accessed December 12, 2007).

Bracey, Gerald. "A Letter to Jonathan Alter of *Newsweek*." *The Huffington Post*, www.huffingtonpost.com (July 7, 2008; accessed July 16).

Brett, Regina. "Students Pass State Test, but at What Cost to Their Education?" *Cleveland Plain Dealer*, July 22, 2008.

Briggs-Myers, Isabel. *The Meyers-Briggs Type Indicator.* Palo Alto, CA: Consulting Psychology Press, 1962.

Briggs-Myers, Isabel, and Mary H. McCauley. *A Guide to the Development and Use of the Myers-Briggs Type Indicator.* Palo Alto, CA: Consulting Psychologists Press, 1989.

Brubacken, John S. *A History of the Problems of Education.* New York: McGraw-Hill, 1966.

Bush, George. "Remarks by the President in Small Business Roundtable." Control Concepts, Pittsburgh, Pennsylvania, February 28, 2001, www.whitehouse.gov/news/releases/2001/02/20010228-10.html.

Cala, William. "High-Stakes Tests Push Kids to Streets." *Rochester Democrat and Chronicle,* July 27, 2008.

California Commission on Teacher Credentialing. California Standards for the Teaching Profession. Adopted January 1997.

California Department of Education and the American Educational Research Association, American Psychological Association, and National Council on Measurement in Education. *California Department of Education STAR Post-Test Guide Version 1-2004, Standards for Educational and Psychological Testing.* March 2004.

Campbell, Peter. Transform Education Blog, http://transformeducation.blogspot.com/2006/01/competition-and-education.html (accessed January 21, 2006).

Canadian Health Network. "School anxiety? What You Can Do to Help Your Child." www.medicalnewstoday.com/articles/12414.php (accessed August 23, 2004).

Cardenas, Tabitha. "One Mother's Story about Test Intimidation." www.susanohanian.org/search_letters.php (accessed March 21, 2008).

Carpenter, Eric. "Teaching Dispute Leads to Parent Picketing and Student Walkout: Reassigned Fourth-Grade Teacher Says She Has History of Student Success, but Doesn't Conform to District Guidelines." *The Orange County Register,* January 2, 2008.

Chang, Timothy, and Daphne Chang. "The Role of Myers-Briggs Type Indicator in Electrical Engineering Education." *ICEE/Proceedings/papers,* 2000.

Cochran-Smith, Marilyn. "Taking Stock in 2006, Evidence, Evidence Everywhere." *Journal of Teacher Education,* Vol. 57, No. 1 (January/February 2006).

Cody, Anthony. "State Schools on Collision Course with Standards." *Fresno Bee,* December 14, 2007, B7.

Cody, Anthony. "Rising Scores May Not Mean Students Are Learning More." *San Jose Mercury News,* Opinion Column, May 1, 2008.

Compton, Mary, and Lois Weiner, eds. *The Global Assault on Teachers, Teaching and Teacher Unions.* New York: Palgrave Macmillan, 2008.

Conway, Martin A., Gillian Cohen, and Nicola Stanhope. "Why Is It That University Grades Do Not Predict Very-Long-Term Retention?" *Journal of Experimental Psychology: General,* Vol. 121, No. 3 (1992).

Cremin, Lawrence A. *Popular Education and Its Discontents.* New York: Harper & Row, 1990.

Darling-Hammond, Linda. "What Is Genuine Accountability?" California Professional Development Consortia, Asilomar, California, November 2009.

Deci, Edward. *Why We Do What We Do: The Dynamics of Personal Autonomy.* New York: Putnam, 1995.

Deming, W. Edwards. *Out of the Crisis.* Cambridge, MA: MIT Press, 1982, 1986.

Desbrow, Marilyn. "Too Much Pressure." *Pasadena Star News,* November 25, 2007.

Dickerson, Bryan. "This Is Only a Test: Are the Stakes Too High for a Flawed System?" *New Times San Luis Obisbo,* August 11, 2005.

Ditka, Mike. Comment during a Cardinals vs. Bears telecast. August 25, 2006.

Doyon , Juanita. "Seattle Teacher Refuses to Administer WASL Test to Students, Citing Multiple Harms Test Causes Students, Teachers, Schools, and Parents." Parent Empowerment Network, Spanaway, Washington, April 20, 2008, www .parentempowermentnetwork.org.

Dunlap, Annette. "Standardized Testing Dumbs Down Education—Today's Over-Tested Students Lack the Genuine Spirit of Inquiry." *Charlotte Observer,* October 27, 2005.

Edmonds, Ron. Kentucky Department of Education web page, www.education .ky.gov/KDE/Instructional+Resources/Closing+the+Gap/ (1973; accessed November 18, 2009).

Ednalino, Percy. "Teacher Won't Administer CSAP Tests." *Denver Post,* January 27, 2001.

Einstein, Albert. *Ideas and Opinions.* New York: Dell, 1981.

Eisner, Elliot W. "The Art and Craft of Teaching." *Educational Leadership,* January 1983.

Emery, Kathy. Part of a panel presentation at the San Francisco State University faculty retreat at Asilomar, California, January 26, 2005, www .educationanddemocracy.org/Emery/Emery_NCLB.htm.

Eysenck, H. J. *The Structure of Human Personality*. London: Methuen, 1953.

Fisher, Marshal. "What's in a Grade." *CSTA Journal*, February 1976.

Freire, Paulo. *Pedagogy of the Oppressed*. New York: Continuum, 1970.

French, Patricia. "Quality—If Its Not Measurable, Does It Matter?" *School of Management Conference Paper*, The Open Polytechnic of New Zealand, 2002.

Garcia, Carlos. "Superintendent of Fresno Unified School District's Vision for Success." Presented at a district-wide meeting, January 14, 1999.

Garrison, Anne E. Levin. "A Second Letter from a Parent." www.susanohanian.org/ show_nclb_atrocities.html?id=2478 (accessed December 7, 2006).

Gassaway, Bernard. "Reflections of an Urban High School Principal." *Education News*, December 12, 2005.

Gersten, Dennis, M.D. "The Modern Oath of Hippocrates." www.imagerynet.com/ hippo.ama.html (1998; accessed November 9, 2009).

Gill, Nancy Ginsburg. "Goodbye, Mr. & Ms. Chips." *Education Week*, July 18, 2007.

Glasser, Robert, Lamar Alexander, and H. Thomas James. "The Nation's Report Card: Improving the Assessment of Student Achievement." *NAEd White Papers*, The National Academy of Education, 1987.

Glovin, David, and David Evans. "How Test Companies Fail Your Kids." *Bloomberg Markets Magazine*, December 1, 2006.

Gonzalez, Juan. "Bronx 8th-Graders Boycott Practice Exam but Teacher May Get Ax." *New York Daily News*, May 21, 2008.

Good, Thomas L. "Teacher Expectations and Student Perceptions: A Decade of Research." *Educational Leadership*, February 1981.

Goodman, Ken. "The Pulse: Education's Place for Debate." www .districtadministration.com/pulse/commentpost.aspx?news=no&postid=47921 (accessed February 5, 2008).

Gould, Stephen Jay. *The Mismeasure of Man*. New York: Norton, 1981.

Gross, Beatrice, and Ronald Gross. *Radical School Reform.* New York: Simon & Schuster, 1970.

Hamel, Catherine Ross, and Fred L. Hamel. "State-Mandated Testing: Why We Opt Out." *Education Week,* March 12, 2003.

Hannan, Kim. Teacher e-mail to Rog Lucido, February 29, 2008.

Hein, George E. (professor emeritus, Lesley University). "Bias in Tests." Posting to ndsgroup@yahoogroups.com, 2007.

Henry, Peter. "The Case against Standardized Testing." *Minnesota English Journal,* December 2007.

Heschong, Lisa. "Windows and Classrooms: A Study of Student Performance and the Indoor Environment." California Energy Commission, P500-03-082-A-7, Heschong Mahone Group, Inc., Fair Oaks, California, September 2003.

Hess, Fredrick M. "The Case for Being Mean." American Enterprise Institute, December 1, 2003, www.frederickhess.org/5049/the-case-for-being-mean.

Hess, Fredrick M., ed. *Educational Entrepreneurship: Realities, Challenges, Possibilities.* Cambridge, MA: Harvard Education Press, 2006.

Hirsh, Sandra, and Jean Kummerow. *Life Types.* New York: Warner Communications, 1989.

Hobson, Emily. "First Things First," www.caljustice.org/cfj_live/images/stories/2003_First_Things_First.pdf (accessed May 17, 2003).

Horn, Jim. "What IS Left Behind?" www.SchoolsMatter.blogspot.com (accessed September 28, 2007).

Humes, Edward. "'No Child Left Behind' Should Really Be Called 'No Test Left Behind.'" Review of *Tested: One American School Struggles to Make the Grade,* by Linda Perlstein. *Los Angeles Times Book Review,* July 9, 2007.

Jehlen, Alain. "Testing: How the Sausage Is Made . . . What's in a Score?" *NEA Today,* January 2007.

Jordan, Michael. "Great Sayings." http://greatsayings.blogspot.com/2006/06/michael-jordan-quotes.html (accessed April 7, 2010).

Jung, C. G. *Psychological Types.* Zurich: Rascher Verlag, 1921.

Kean, Michael H. "No Single Test Does Everything—The Importance of Multiple Measures." CTB/McGraw-Hill, www.maths456.net/wbja/html/48860.html (accessed December 29, 2004).

Keirsey, David, and Marilyn Bates. *Please Understand Me.* Del Mar, CA: Prometheus Nemesis Book Company, 1978.

"Key Elements of Testing/Test Measurement Principles." California Department of Education, May 2004, www.cde.ca.gov/ta/tg/sa/documents/keyelements0504.pdf

Knowledge Networks. "AP Poll," Menlo Park, CA. http://surveys.ap.org/data/KnowledgeNetworks/AP%20Education%20Poll%20Topline%2006-24-08.pdf (accessed June 23, 2008).

Kohn, Alfie. *The Case against Standardized Testing.* Portsmouth, NH: Heinemann, 2000.

Kovacs, Philip. "Gates, Buffett, and the Corporatization of Children." Common Dreams, www.commondreams.org/views06/0628-30.htm (accessed June 28, 2006).

Kuehn, Larry. "Schools for Globalized Business: The APEC Agenda for Education." Commentary on the "Concept Paper" for the APEC Human Resources Ministerial Meeting. *Corpwatch*, British Columbia Teachers' Federation, May 1, 1997.

Lawrence, Gordon. *People Types & Tiger Stripes.* Gainesville, FL: Center for Application of Psychological Type, 1979.

Leonard, George B. *Education and Ecstacy.* New York: Delacorte Press, 1968.

Long, Cindy. "Can We Compete? In the Face of New Global Rivalries, the Answer Is Still Yes—And American Math and Science Education Has the World Watching." *NEA Today*, January 2007.

Lowell, Lindsay, and Harold Salzman. "Assessing the Evidence on Science and Engineering Education, Quality, and Workforce Demand." The Urban Institute, www.urban.org/publications/411562.html (accessed October, 2007).

Magnuson, Peter. "High-Stakes Cheating: Will the Focus on Accountability Lead to More Cheating?" *Communicator*, February 2000.

Majoy, Peter. "Thread III—NCLB's Ideological Underpinning." Assessment Reform Network List posting e-mail (accessed August 27, 2005).

"Making Teens Start School in the Morning Is 'Cruel,' Brain Doctor Claims." *London Evening Standard*, June 10, 2008, www.thisislondon.co.uk/news/ article-23381421.

Marefat, Fahimeh. "Student Writing, Personality Type of the Student and Rater: Any Interrelationship?" *The Reading Matrix*, Vol. 6, No. 2 (September 2006).

Mathis, William J. "The Clarity of a Mother's Voice." *Rutland Herald*, January 17, 2008.

McIntosh, Don. "Schools' 'Broad' Agenda." *Willamette Week Online*, May 5, 2005, www.wweek.com/editorial/3226/7507 (accessed May 5, 2005).

McNeil, L. M., E. Coppola, J. Radigan, and J. Vasquez Heilig. "Avoidable Losses: High-Stakes Accountability and the Dropout Crisis." *Education Policy Analysis Archives*, January 2008.

Messick, S. *Educational Measurement*, third ed. New York: Macmillan, 1989.

Miller, Jacob. "MCAS Hinders Student Learning" (letter to the editor). *South Coast Today*, October 9, 2007.

Miner, Barbara. "For-Profits Target Education." *Rethinking Schools*, Spring 2002.

Murray, Charles. "Acid Tests: No Child Left Behind Is Uninformative. It Is Deceptive." *Wall Street Journal*, July 25, 2006.

National Commission for the Protection of Human Subjects of Biomedical and Behavioral Research. "National Research Act of 1974." Public Law 93-348, July 1974.

National Commission on Excellence in Education. *A Nation at Risk*. Washington, DC: U.S. Government Printing Office, 1983.

Neil, Monty. "McClellan Tell-All Exposes Media's Propaganda Problem." Assessment Reform Network Listserv e-mail (accessed June 14, 2008).

O'Connell, Jack. "Schools Chief Jack O'Connell Announces Proposed Changes to California's NCLB Accountability Workbook." News Release: #04-18, February 25, 2004.

Ohanian, Susan. "Weep for Our Profession: The Corporate Politicos Are Killing It, Scene: Wake County Schools, One of the 20 Largest Districts in the U.S." North Carolina teacher's e-mail, September 12, 2007.

Ohanian, Susan. *When Childhood Collides with NCLB.* Brandon, VT: Vermont Society for the Study of Education, 2008.

Popham, W. James. *The Truth about Testing.* Alexandria, VA: ASCD, 2001.

Posner, Dave. "Bubble Students and Teaching to the Statistic." *San Jose Mercury News,* March 23, 2001.

Poyner, Leslie, and Paula M. Wolfe. *Marketing Fear in America's Public Schools.* Mahwah, NJ: Lawrence Erlbaum Associates, 2004.

Pratt, Linda K. "The Relationship of the Myers-Briggs Type Indicator to Scores on the National Teacher's Examination." American Institute of Research Forum Paper, 1981.

Prevost, Jean-Pierre. "What Is All This Murmuring About?" *God's Word Today,* June 2008.

Public School Insights. "Greenway Elementary: Empowering Educators to Close the Achievement Gap." 2008, www.publicschoolinsights.org/greenway-elementary-empowering-educators-close-achievement-gap.

Puett, Glenda. "A Teacher's Note." www.susanohanian.org/show_atrocities .html?id=7959 (accessed April 15, 2008).

Renteria, Esperanza. "Teaching to Change L.A.: An Educational Bill of Rights." *Online Journal for IDEA,* Vol. 2, Issue 3, No. 1–10, www.tcla.gseis.ucla.edu/rights/ features/3/student/acosta3.html (accessed March 11, 2002).

Rogers, Carl R. *Freedom to Learn.* Columbus, OH: Charles Merrill, 1969.

Rotberg, Iris C. "Quick Fixes, Test Scores, and the Global Economy—Myths That Continue to Confound Us." *Ed Week,* Vol. 27, Issue 41 (June 11, 2008).

Rothstein , Richard. "Leaving NCLB Behind." *American Prospect,* www.prospect.org/ cs/articles?article=leaving_nclb_behind (accessed December 17, 2007).

Rothstein, Richard. "Whose Problem Is Poverty?" *Educational Leadership,* Vol. 65, No. 7 (April 2008).

Rowland Unified School District. "No Excuses University." 2009, www .rowlandschools.org/apps/news/show_news.jsp?REC_ID=110742&id=0.

Schultz, Elizabeth. "Enemy of Innovation— Our Obsession with Standardized Testing Is Impeding Reform." *Teacher Magazine,* September 1992.

Schulz, Greta. "Economic Uncertainty or Excuse-Making?" *St. Louis Business Journal*, http://atlanta.bizjournals.com/stlouis/stories/2008/03/03/smallb2 .html?page=2 (accessed February 29, 2008).

Shaker, Paul. "Business, Conscience, and Teaching." *Ed Week*, January 9, 2008.

Sloan, Chris. "Students Are People, Not Numbers: What Will It Take to Get Teachers to Refuse to Participate in a System That Harms Children?" *The San Angelo Standard-Times*, March 4, 2008.

Sloan, Richard P. "The Critical Distinction between Science and Religion." In *Blind Faith: The Unholy Alliance of Religion and Medicine*. New York: St. Martin's Press, 2006.

Smithsonian Staff. "Inventors." *Smithsonian*, July 19, 1988.

Standardized Testing and Reporting (STAR) Program. "Explaining 2008 STAR Program Student Reports to Parents and Guardians." www.cde.ca.gov/ta/tg/sr/ documents/explnrpts08.pdf (accessed November 10, 2009).

Stansbury, Meris. "U.S. Educators Seek Lessons from Scandinavia High Scoring Nations on an International Exam Say Success Stems from Autonomy, Project-Based Learning." *eSchool News*, www.eschoolnews.com/news/top-news/?i=52770 (accessed March 3, 2008).

Staff. "Individual Acts of Resistance." *FairTest Examiner*, July 11, 2008.

Staff. "Teacher Defies Test Rule." *New York Times*, July 15, 1998.

Steffenhagen, Janet. "Teacher in Hot Water Over Not Giving Test—Colleagues Plan to Rally in Support of Educator." *Vancouver Sun*, September 25, 2007.

Stiggins, Rick. "Educational Testing Service's Assessment Training Institute." *Ed Week*, Vol. 27, Issue 8 (October 17, 2007).

Strauss, Steve. "Teachers Stand Up against Cookie-Cutter Education." *Freedom Socialist*, Vol. 27, No. 5 (October–November 2006).

Strauss, Valerie. "The Rise of the Testing Culture: As Exam-Takers Get Younger, Some Say Value Is Overblown." *Washington Post*, October 10, 2006.

Thorndike, Robert L., and Elizabeth Hogan. *Measurement and Evaluation in Psychology and Education*. New York: John Wiley, 1961.

Tienken, Christopher H. "Rankings of International Achievement, Test Performance, and Economic Strength: Correlation or Conjecture?" *International Journal of Education Policy & Leadership*, Vol. 3, No. 4 (April 25, 2008).

Wadhwa, Vivek. "The Science Education Myth: Forget the Conventional Wisdom. U.S. Schools Are Turning Out More Capable Science and Engineering Grads than the Job Market Can Support." *Viewpoint, Business Week*, October 26, 2007, www.urban.org/publications/411562.html, or www.businessweek .com/smallbiz/content/oct2007/sb20071025_827398.htm (accessed November 23, 2009).

Wallis, Claudia. "No Child Left Behind—Doomed to Fail." *Time Magazine*, June 8, 2008.

Western Association of Schools and Colleges Accrediting Commission for Schools. "Why WASC?" www.acswasc.org/about_why.htm (accessed October 20, 2009).

Williams, Bronwyn T. "Standardized Students: The Problems with Writing for Tests Instead of People." *Journal of Adolescent & Adult Literacy*, Vol. 49, No. 2 (October 2005).

Williams, Juliet. "School Districts Face Sanctions." *Associated Press*, January 15, 2008.

Winerip, Michael. "Are Schools Passing or Failing? Now There's a Third Choice . . . Both." *New York Times*, November 2, 2005.

World Economic Forum. "Global Competitiveness Report Country Profile Highlights 2007/2008." www.weforum.org/en/initiatives/gcp/Global%20Competit iveness%20Report/Highlights2008/index.htm (accessed November 20, 2009).

Zweifel, Dave. "Teacher Shows Folly of No Child." *The Capital Times*, November 7, 2007.

About the Author

Horace (Rog) Lucido has taught physics and mathematics for over thirty-eight years in both private and public schools. He graduated from St. Mary's College, Moraga, California, with a B.S. in physics/mathematics and did graduate work in physics at both San Diego State University and University of California, Berkeley. He is a certified program evaluator and Meyers-Briggs presenter. He was past vice-president of the Northern California Section of the American Association of Physics Teachers. He was both a mentor and master teacher for Fresno State University as well as Fresno Pacific University. He helped plan the Center for Advanced Research and Technology and taught there as well. He authored *Test, Grade, and Score—Never More*, published articles in the *Physics Teacher Magazine*, and served as contributor/consultant to *Conceptual Physics*. He has given numerous workshops on "coaching in the classroom" as well as "forgiving learning" using mastery conferences. He was one of the founding members of Educators and Parents Against Testing Abuse (EPATA) and the Chavez Education Conference, and is the Central Valley coordinator of the Assessment Reform Network. He currently is an adjunct instructor at Heald College.

Breinigsville, PA USA
20 July 2010
242082BV00002B/6/P